SAGA OF THE AMERICAN FLAG

SAGA OF THE AMERICAN FLAG

★ ═══════════════════════════════════ ★

An Illustrated History

by Candice M. DeBarr (Marie) and Jack A. Bonkowske [1941]

───────────────── ★ ─────────────────

Flag illustrations by Barbara Schiefer
Scenic illustrations by Antonio Castro

HARBINGER HOUSE
Tucson ★ New York

Harbinger House, Inc.
Tucson, Arizona

Copyright © 1990 by Candice M. DeBarr and Jack A. Bonkowske

Flag illustrations copyright © 1990 by Barbara Schiefer

Scenic illustrations copyright © 1990 by Antonio Castro

Designed by Rebecca Gaver

Manufactured in the United States of America

Library of Congress Cataloging-in-Publication Data

DeBarr, Candice M. (Candice Marie), 1941 –
    Saga of the American flag : an illustrated history / by Candice M.
DeBarr and Jack A. Bonkowske : flag illustrations by Barbara
Schiefer : scenic illustrations by Antonio Castro.
        p.   cm.
    Includes bibliographical references.
    Summary: Traces, in text and illustrations, the evolution of the
United States flag.
    ISBN 0-943173-65-5 : $9.95
    1. Flags — United States — History.   [1. Flags — United States —
— History.]   I. Bonkowske, Jack A. (Jack Albert), 1936 — .
II. Schiefer, Barbara, 1945 —   ill.   III. Castro, Antonio, 1941 —
ill.   IV. Title.
CR113.D38   1990
929.9'2'0973 — dc20   89-26805

CONTENTS

INTRODUCTION

THE CLASHING OF SWORDS, the screams of wounded and dying men and horses, and the cries of orders from both sides of the battle split the normally serene desert surroundings. The sweet smell of spilled blood mixed with the churning dust hangs in the oppressive heat. A large black horse carrying a standard-bearer rears violently, a spear protruding from his heavily muscled chest. He collapses, his last tremor of life slipping away with that of his mortally wounded rider.

As one man, five soldiers turn to their fallen comrade. The first man to reach the corpse leans over his mount's neck, grasping for the staff holding the standard of his sovereign. Too late, his eye catches the arcing flash of a blade, and his head rolls under the hooves of the horses behind him. Again the soldiers reach for the staff; again a sword wields its death blow. The grim battle rages on, each side intent on the standard quivering among the growing heap of corpses at its base.

With a triumphant yell, a young soldier, barely old enough to leave his mother's side, grasps the pole with a bloodied hand. He spurs his mount savagely and races for a sandy knoll, the standard held high. Today's battle is over. Tomorrow the men, joined by others, will follow their standard into yet another contest for power.

Centuries later, a large gathering of soldiers stands silently. All eyes watch the flagpole in the center of the formation. Slowly the flag is lowered. Two uniformed men step forward to catch the tattered silk. The material is folded with care while a bright, new flag is raised in its place. As the flag reaches the top of the pole, a gust of wind snaps the cloth to its full length, displaying the colors clearly against the blue sky. A cheer rises from most of the onlookers, drowning out the sobs and angry cries of the defeated who are watching their leader place the symbol of their country into the hands of the victor.

Pieces of material sewn together to form a design. Created by man, it is an object with no life of its own. Yet, throughout history, men and women have given their lives for it; poems, songs and stories have sung its praises; children have been taught to revere it; and hardened men have broken down in tears at the sight of it. It is called a flag.

THE HISTORY OF FLAGS

Whaт is a flag? Webster's *New World Dictionary of the American Language* defines it as "a piece of cloth or bunting, often attached to a staff, with distinctive colors, patterns, or symbolic devices, used as a national or state symbol, to signal, etc.; banner; standard; ensign."

Does this definition encompass the meaning of a flag, or explain the powerful emotions it evokes in mankind? The answer, of course, depends upon what type of flag is being discussed and by whom.

A flag is a symbol. It represents people united by a common bond or cause. This bond could be organizational, military, state, religious or national. The flag is often used as a rallying point. It should be a source of pride, for a flag encompasses the hopes and ideals of the people it represents.

The earliest recorded symbols used to represent a person or people were standards. The standard was mounted on a pole or spear and thrust into the ground to signify a person or group's territory. Later, the standard was carried into battle to aid in identification. Standards were in existence thousands of years ago, and history shows us they were made from various materials, including animal skins, carved wood, stone and even metal. The standard is still used in place of the flag, particularly in youth organizations and some foreign countries.

The first forms resembling modern flags were banners. They were made of cloth and displayed on a staff, and their main function was to indicate a person of importance such as a king, a duke or a military leader. Banners were mentioned in the Bible during the days of Solomon more than 3,000 years ago! While these banners could have a religious meaning, they were not used to signify a group of people, their territory or a nation.

During the Middle Ages, a number of independent city-states in Italy, in a quest for an individual symbol of identity, were the first to use an extension of the banner as a symbol that would represent them. Thus, the concept of the flag as we know it was born.

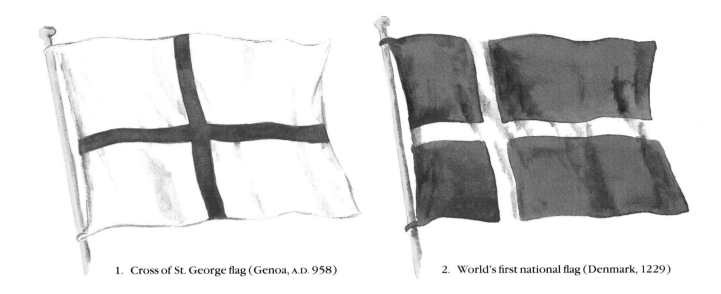

1. Cross of St. George flag (Genoa, A.D. 958)   2. World's first national flag (Denmark, 1229)

One of these city-states, Genoa, was founded in A.D. 958. Genoa's flag was referred to as the Cross of St. George, a simply designed flag made up of a white background with a red cross (*Illustration 1*). The flag was surrounded by a romantic myth concerning a certain Roman soldier who (sometime around the year A.D. 200) converted to Christianity, slew a dragon and died a martyr to his religion.

In about A.D. 1100, Genoa was visited by the English Crusaders. The Crusaders were so taken by the flag and its legend that they took both back to England. The Cross of St. George gradually replaced the other banners used throughout England and became the symbol of the country that played a major part in the colonization of what was to become the United States of America.

Flags became an accepted form of communicating associations, religions, kingdoms, armies, etc. The designs were as varied as the people the symbols represented.

While the Cross of St. George was accepted as the flag of England, there is no evidence that it was the official flag of the land. The first national flag is believed to have belonged to Denmark. Consisting of a red background and white cross, it flew during the rule of King Waldemar I in 1229 and is still the official flag of Denmark — more than 750 years later (*Illustration 2*).

During the days of the Cross of St. George flag, Scotland was using a flag known as the Cross of St. Andrew. The Cross of St. Andrew consisted of a blue field with a white diagonal cross (*Illustration 3*).

3. Cross of St. Andrew flag (Scotland)

In 1606, King James of England united England and Scotland. Because neither the Scots nor the English would honor the other's flag, King James decreed that the flags, as well as the two countries, would merge. This decree not only created the first rendition of the Union flag by combining the crosses of St. Andrew and St. George on one field, it also gave England its first recorded official flag. The Union flag was to remain unchanged for the next 195 years, between 1606 and 1801 (*Illustration 4*).

4. First Union flag (England, Scotland, 1606)

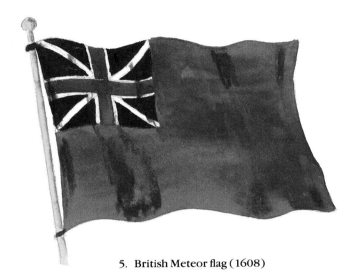

5.   British Meteor flag (1608)

But the new Union flag was hard to see from a distance when flown aboard British ships. To make identification of British ships easier at a distance and during the heat of battle, a new naval flag was introduced about 1608. The Meteor flag had a bright red field with the crosses of St. George and St. Andrew in the canton, the upper left corner (*Illustration 5*). The Red Ensign flag was also designed. This flag also had a bright red field. However, the white canton displayed only the cross of St. George (*Illustration 6*).

6.   British Red Ensign flag

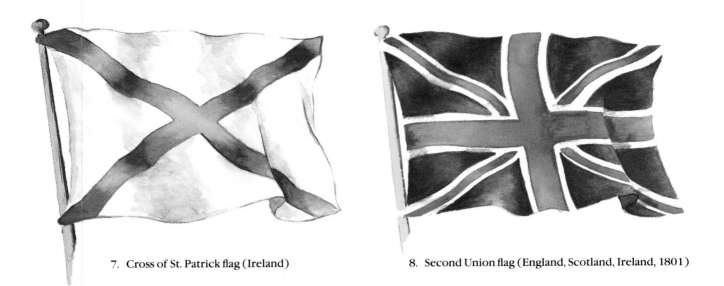

7. Cross of St. Patrick flag (Ireland)   8. Second Union flag (England, Scotland, Ireland, 1801)

In 1801, Ireland became a part of Great Britain. As with Scotland, the national flags, as well as the countries, merged and the second Union flag of England was conceived. England's Union flag now consisted of the Irish Cross of St. Patrick (*Illustration 7*), Scotland's Cross of St. Andrew and England's Cross of St. George on a common field of blue. This flag is still in use (*Illustration 8*).

Because the United States is a direct offspring of Great Britain, the histories of their flags are closely related. The American Colonies and the British used the same flags for almost 150 years — both on land and on sea.

EARLY AMERICAN FLAGS ★ 2

THE AMERICAN FLAG was not designed, sewn and accepted by the colonists without its trials. The American flag, as we know it today, went through a long period of many changes before becoming the Stars and Stripes. Even after the flag became the official symbol of the rebellious new country, few were alike in size, color or even design.

The forerunners of flags in America were symbols (standards) used by Indian tribes. Although some tribes were identified by their physical appearance, many had developed standards much like those used in Europe and Asia thousands of years before.

These standards were often a symbol of the tribes' "animal god," which was believed to be watching over them and lending "his" spirit to the members of "his" tribe. These symbols were made of leather, wood, stone and so on, and often decorated with feathers and/or stained in different colors to create a distinctive standard that was placed on a spear or lance. The "flag" was carried by the chief or his emissary during battle and was placed in a conspicuous position during times of peace.

Some Native American tribes also used another type of standard known as the totem pole. Usually a tall wooden carving, sometimes decorated with feathers and stained various colors, a totem was too large to be carried and was, therefore, a stationary standard (*Illustration 9*).

It is generally accepted that the first real flag flown in what would become the United States was a white flag with a black raven on it (*Illustration 10*). Legend tells us this flag was carried by Erik the Red and his son, Leif Eriksson, Viking explorers believed to have landed in the Americas during A.D. 1000.

There are no actual illustrations or consistently accurate written descriptions to prove the existence of the Viking flag. However, coins of the early ninth century show a fringed, triangular flag, sometimes with a cross in the

9. Totem pole

10. Viking flag of Leif Eriksson (A.D. 1000)

field and sometimes with a raven. A flag already in use at the time the St. George flag was introduced? No one can be certain. It is fact, however, that the Vikings raided England's shores during that time.

If the Viking flag (white with a black raven) did exist — and the majority of our historians accept that it did — it is doubtful the flag represented the Vikings as a nation. The Bayeux tapestry, an embroidery made between A.D. 1070 and 1080, shows us that flags were commonly used, but not as national symbols. The Viking flag, therefore, would most likely have been a personal flag of Erik and his son, Leif.

The next flag to fly over American soil was the Spanish flag, brought to the New World by Christopher Columbus in 1492. Throughout the 1500s, the Spanish flag was the predominant flag in the Americas. Ponce de Leon claimed Florida for Spain in 1513, and the Spanish flag flew there until 1763 (*Illustration 11*).

11. Spanish flag

12. French flag

The British flag made its first appearance in the New World in 1497 when John Cabot claimed much of the Atlantic coast for England.

In 1534, the Frenchman Jacques Cartier sailed up the St. Lawrence between the United States and Canada and claimed nearly half of the North American continent for France (*Illustration 12*).

13. Dutch flag   14. Swedish flag

Another Englishman, Henry Hudson, brought the Dutch flag into what is now the New York harbor in 1609 and founded the Providence of New Netherlands in 1623, claiming both to be under Dutch law (*Illustration 13*).

During the same period, a Dutchman by the name of Peter Minuit, working for the chartered West India Company, purchased Manhattan Island from the Indians and founded New Amsterdam. Minuit left the Dutch colony in 1628, organized the New Sweden Company, and founded a Swedish colony on the Delaware River about 10 years later. This settlement is now known as Wilmington, Delaware. The Swedish flag, a gold cross on a blue (*Illustration 14*) flew over the colony until 1655 when Peter Stuyvesant, the governor of New Netherlands, marched on the small colony, struck the Swedish flag and replaced it with the Dutch flag.

In 1664, an English task force assumed control of Stuyvesant's colonies (the New Netherlands and the acquired Swedish colony). The Dutch flag was lowered. When the Union flag was raised, the New Netherlands colony became known as New York. England and France were left to solidify their claims over the majority of the North American continent as Spain built its strength in the South and West.

The nationalities of people who settled in the New World were not necessarily represented by the flags that flew over their settlements. While it is true that many of them came to this country to escape political or religious persecution, others were sponsored by a country or a private company. This sponsorship was a business proposition; in exchange for the colonists' passage, a payment in the form of tobacco, furs, and precious metals was expected by their sponsors. And it was not unusual for a settlement to be overtaken by a

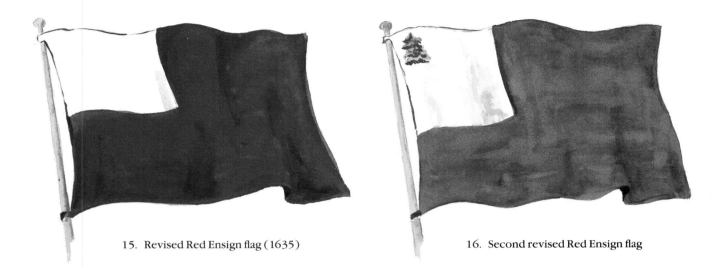

15. Revised Red Ensign flag (1635)

16. Second revised Red Ensign flag

colony under another country's rule. Thus began the mixing of different nationalities and customs, which was to become the strength of this new country as she fought for freedom and recognition.

The American flag's forerunner, England's Union Jack, was flown at Jamestown, Virginia (1607), and Plymouth, Massachusetts (1620), while the naval flags continued to be the Red Ensign and the Meteor flags.

However, the Puritans of Massachusetts strongly objected to the use of the cross in the canton of the British Red Ensign. In 1635, they had the cross removed, leaving a red flag with an empty white canton and making it the first recorded change of an offiicial British flag to suit the colonists' purpose (*Illustration 15*). This flag was used on land and sea for 50 years or more, after which the cross was restored, but with a pine tree, signifying liberty, in the upper left-hand corner of the canton (*Illustration 16*).

During the 1700s several colonial flags were used in addition to the English flags. They usually were naval ensigns identifying a trade or company. For example, New York shippers used a white flag with a black beaver on it, symbolizing the fur trade (*Illustration 17*). The New England pine tree was on several flags and exists on the back of the Massachusetts state flag today.

The French and Indian War, also known as the Seven Years' War (1756 to 1763), united the British and the American colonists in a common cause. At the war's end, the British found themselves financially strapped. In an effort to recoup some of their losses, the British turned to their colonies for financial relief. The colonists resented the increased tariffs and other changes imposed by the "mother country." Resentment broke out in many forms, such as the Boston Tea Party.

17. New York shippers' flag (1700s)

Subtle forms of rebellion included unflattering additions to the Union Jack. American patriots in militias and other military organizations began flying flags of their own design. Often these flags depicted a reptile native to the New World — the rattlesnake — coiled or stretched across the field, with the words "Don't Tread On Me" (*Illustration 18*). Many used the New England pine tree and various mottos. When the Revolutionary War began, the addition of both symbols to the Union Jack was widespread.

The first flag to use 13 stripes to symbolize the 13 colonies is presumed to be the Markoe flag. It was a yellow flag with a coat of arms in the center containing 13 blue and silver stripes in the canton (*Illustration 19*).

18. "Don't Tread On Me" flag

19. Markoe flag

20. United Train of Artillery flag (1775)

21. First Rhode Island Regiment flag

The first flag to symbolize the colonies by using 13 stars is believed to be that used by a military battery of Providence, Rhode Island, called the United Train of Artillery and organized in 1775. The field was yellow with a fouled anchor, two cannons, scrolls with mottos and a coiled rattlesnake circled by 13 blue five-pointed stars (*Illustration 20*). This flag has been preserved and is on display at the Historical Society Museum in Providence.

Another pre-Revolutionary War flag using the 13 stars to symbolize the original colonies was carried by the First Rhode Island Regiment. A white flag, it contained a blue canton with 13 stars (*Illustration 21*). This flag has also been preserved and can be seen at the statehouse.

These were only a few of the many flags used by the colonists before and during the early part of the Revolutionary War.

THE STARS AND STRIPES ★ 3

O N JULY 3, 1775, George Washington began forming the first Continental Army. His "troops" came from towns, rural settlements and farms. Yet even the individual farmer usually belonged to the militia headquartered in the nearest settlement or town, and it was these many militias that formed much of the first U.S. Army. It must have been a colorful sight as one militia after another arrived, some with full or partial uniforms of their own design and color, and all carrying their own individually designed flags!

On January 1, 1776, the Continental Army was formed, and a common flag was hoisted on a flagstaff 76 feet in height (a ship's mast) set on Prospect Hill in Boston. The flag was a British Meteor flag with six horizontal white stripes added across the red field. It was hailed as the Grand Union flag (*Illustration 22*). It was also later called the Cambridge flag and the Continental flag. While its origin is unknown and it was never officially approved, it was widely used aboard ships until July 4, 1776. There is no record of its being carried into battle on land.

After the signing of the Declaration of Independence, the Grand Union flag became obsolete and was used less and less. Its last recorded use on land was at Fort Schuyler, New York, in August of 1777.

On June 14, 1777, Congress passed a short resolution:

> Resolved: that the flag of the United States be made of thirteen
> stripes, alternate red and white; that the union be thirteen stars
> white in a blue field, representing a new constellation.

The resolution did not define the proportions of the new Stars and Stripes. Nor did it state the direction of the stripes, size of the canton, the design or arrangement of the stars or, in fact, the size of the flag itself. It did not say why the colors red, white and blue were chosen. Consequently, the flag

22. Grand Union flag (1776)

23. *Alliance* flag

makers were free to make the national flag to their own liking. It was not until 41 years later that Congress specified the stripes would be horizontal. Complete official specifications for the design of the flag were not defined until 1912, and then not by Congress, but by an executive order of President William Howard Taft.

Following custom, the flag was flown mainly by ships. Permanent fortresses were the only places on land displaying the flag. Therefore, even though Congress had officially designated a flag for its country, it seems to have been intended for marine or naval use, and not for use in battle on land. Further substantiating this premise is the fact that the Stars and Stripes was not issued to the U.S. Army by Congress until after the Revolutionary War.

The Stars and Stripes was, however, issued to the Continental Navy during the Revolutionary War. The first documented use shows it to have been flown from a U.S. ship on or before November 1, 1777, under the command of John Paul Jones. The flag was also flying from the mast of a U.S. ship during the first capture of an enemy ship at sea — again under the command of Jones.

On February 14, 1778, Jones received a nine-gun salute from the French at Quiberon Bay, the highest honor the French government allowed a foreign vessel. The Stars and Stripes was flying from the mast, making it the first flag to represent the United States in a foreign port, and the first flag to receive recognition as representing the United States as a nation.

Jones was also involved in an episode leading to one of the first artistic renditions of the original Stars and Stripes. After capturing the British ship *Serapis* and leaving his own *Bon Homme Richard* sinking, Jones, accompanied by the American ship *Alliance*, reached Texel in the Netherlands on October 3, 1779. The British ambassador demanded that the Dutch seize

24. *Serapis* flag   25. Bennington flag (1777)

Jones, his ships and their crews, charging them with piracy. The Dutch had an artist draw the flags of each ship. The first drawing shows *Alliance* flying the Stars and Stripes. The second depicts the captured *Serapis* flying Jones' rendition of the American flag.

Alliance's flag is longer than its width. It has seven white and six red stripes with the canton sitting on top of the seventh stripe. The stars have eight points and are arranged in rows of three, two, three, two and three for a total of 13 stars (*Illustration 23*).

The flag on the *Serapis* is a little longer than wide, with the canton on top of the sixth stripe. However, the stripes are red, white and blue. The canton is small, with 13 eight-pointed white stars in three rows — four, five and four. The stripes do not seem to have any particular order as far as color placement is concerned (*Illustration 24*).

Both of these paintings are at the Chicago Historical Society.

This episode was but one showing the various interpretations of Congress' resolution stating the design of the U.S. flag. According to the paintings of the times, some marine flags even had vertical stripes!

Approximately ten years after John Paul Jones had taken the Stars and Stripes to Europe, Captain James Cook introduced the flag to Asia while trying to find the Northwest Passage around North America. During his endeavors (1776-1779), he made surveys showing he had visited Canton, China, on his last trip before being killed by natives in the Hawaiian Islands on February 14, 1779.

The first man credited with taking the Stars and Stripes around the world is Captain Robert Gray. He sailed the *Columbia* out of Boston in 1787, flying the Stars and Stripes while retracing the trip to the northwest coast for a load of furs. From there he sailed to Canton, China, trading furs for tea, and returned home on August 6, 1790, thus completing a 42,000-mile trip.

Although the Stars and Stripes was not given to the Continental Army until 1783, claims have been made that a form of the flag was flown even before the flag resolution of June 14, 1777. Unfortunately, there is no solid evidence to back up those claims.

Some authorities assume the Battle of Bennington to be the site of the first appearance of the Stars and Stripes in a land battle. The battle took place August 16, 1777, on the New York–Vermont border. The flag is preserved in the Bennington, New York, historical museum and is the oldest Stars and Stripes in existence. It was originally owned by Nathaniel Fillmore, grandfather of Millard Fillmore, America's 13th president.

The Bennington flag is an unofficial flag. It has an unusual design — seven white stripes and six red stripes with an extremely large canton. The canton is blue, half the length of the flag, with only four stripes below it. It has 13 seven-pointed white stars. Eleven stars form an arch around the numerals 76, also in white. The two remaining stars are in the upper corners of the canton. The flag is ten feet long by five and a half feet wide (*Illustration 25*).

Other claims to the use of the Stars and Stripes (after the June 4, 1777, congressional resolution) during a battle on land were connected to the Battle of Coach's Bridge, Delaware, on September 3, 1777, and the Battle of Brandywine, Pennsylvania, on September 11, 1777. While it is indeed possible a flag conforming to Congress' resolution did fly during both of these battles, no evidence exists to prove it.

Our southern states claim the Stars and Stripes was first flown during a battle on land in North Carolina, at the Battle of Guilford Courthouse on March 15, 1781. This flag, also referred to as the North Carolina Militia flag, is

26. North Carolina Militia flag (1781)

27. Third Mountain Regiment flag (1781)

preserved at the Hall of History in Raleigh, N.C. While the flag conforms to the criteria set by Congress insofar as it has 13 red and blue stripes — its canton is white with large blue stars. Because of the color placement, it does not conform with the flag resolution of June 14, 1777 (*Illustration 26*).

South Carolina claims a Stars and Stripes, complying with the Congressional Flag Resolution of 1777, was carried into battle by the Third Mountain Regiment on January 17, 1781, at Cowpens, South Carolina. True, the flag has 13 alternate red and white stripes (seven red and six white), the canton is blue and it contains 13 white stars (five-pointed) placed in a circle of 12 stars surrounding one star. On that basis, the Third Mountain Regiment flag does conform to the June 14, 1777, resolution. But this was a regimental flag and not necessarily an official flag for the colonies (*Illustration 27*).

Another form of the Stars and Stripes was present at the surrender of the British General Charles Cornwallis at Yorktown, Virginia, on October 19, 1781, and was documented by several people present. Lieutenant Colonel John Graves Simcoe did a painting of the siege at Yorktown, showing the Stars and Stripes flying with a blue union containing rows of stars that appear to be yet a darker blue. A flag of the same description was referred to in a diary kept by Sergeant George Tucker. A mercenary with the British army recorded that a large flag with 13 stripes was present. But, as with the North Carolina Militia flag, the color placement did not conform with the June 14, 1777, resolution.

These documentations give evidence that various designs or interpretations of the Stars and Stripes were flown or carried during battle on land in the Revolutionary War. But one must remember that no official flag was sent to Washington and his Continental Army until 1783. Therefore, none of the flags used so far can be taken as the official flag of the United States.

4

LEGENDS SURROUNDING THE FIRST OFFICIAL FLAG

SEVERAL LEGENDS surround the first American flag. Perhaps the best known and most widely accepted is that of Betsy Ross. Legend tells of George Washington, George Ross and Robert Morris being appointed in June 1776 to design a national flag. Supposedly, Washington made a crude design that was dispatched to Betsy Ross, widow of George Ross's nephew and an expert seamstress, in Philadelphia. Taking the rough sketch and changing only the number of points on the stars from six to five, Mrs. Ross cut and sewed the first national flag for the United States.

History tells us Betsy Ross was a twice-widowed seamstress who may have made some navy flags. While it is documented that Washington was in Philadelphia for two weeks in 1776, the trip was made on urgent military business. It is doubtful he would have had time to design a flag and, in fact, there is no evidence of his being ordered to do so. Also, the Betsy Ross story was first told in 1870, 94 years after it supposedly took place. The story has all the proper ingredients — hurried meetings, hasty sketches, patriotic widow sewing the new nation's flag for the country her late husband died defending. However, history has proven it to be just a story.

Another legend concerns a captain of a minuteman company, John Hulbert. According to Hulbert's supporters, he made the original Stars and Stripes in 1775, a full year before Betsy Ross. The only evidence supporting this claim is the fact that in 1926 a ragged flag was found in a house Hulbert once lived in. It looked very much like an original. However, Hulbert had kept a detailed diary from 1770 to 1805 and there was no mention of his making a flag.

28. Easton, Pennsylvania, flag (1812)

The Easton, Pennsylvania, flag, a reverse of the national flag, with 13 red and white stripes in the canton and white stars in a field of blue, was carried during the War of 1812 (*Illustration 28*). About 1900 it was promoted as being the first Stars and Stripes. A story was written, making it the flag at Easton on July 8, 1776. The story gave no description of the flag except to mention it had a symbol relating to the original 13 colonies. Again, little, if any, evidence supports its claim of being the first official flag.

Perhaps Francis Hopkinson, a signer of the Declaration of Independence, has the only documented public claim to being the designer and maker of the original U.S. flag. Hopkinson was a congressman, a chairman of a three-man Navy board, the Treasurer of Loans for the United States, and a judge in Pennsylvania. He submitted a claim stating that he was responsible for:

> The flag of the United States of America, seven devices for Continental Currency, a Seal for the Board of Treasury, Great Seal of the United States of America with Reverse.

As payment, he asked for a "quarter cask of public wine." Payment would have documented Francis Hopkinson as maker of the first flag, but no payment was made. A formal bill was later sent to Congress on August 23, 1781. It also was refused. While it is possible that Hopkinson may have been involved with the design of the original Stars and Stripes, historians agree it is doubtful he was the sole designer.

Yet another group has traced the design of the Stars and Stripes back to the 1500s in England. Lawrence Washington, an ancestor of George Washington, was Lord of Gulgrane Manor in 1539. The Washington coat of arms consisted of a silver shield with two red bars and three red five-pointed stars, crested with a raven (*Illustration 29*). Any relationship between the earlier Washington coat of arms and the much later Stars and Stripes flag representing the United States is generally accepted as pure speculation. When one considers the mood of the colonists toward the English in 1777, the idea of an English nobility crest being adapted for the first national flag for the new nation appears highly unlikely.

29. Washington coat of arms

The origins of the Stars and Stripes are shrouded in mystery, legends and half-truths. Facts strongly suggest that the flag had no single designer but was a conglomeration of ideas and designs. Any claim that the Stars and Stripes was used before June 14, 1777, is without verification. No flag has ever been found that conformed to Congress' Flag Resolution of 1777, nor documented proof of one's existence. It is also unlikely that any official Stars and Stripes flag ever flew the year following the signing of the Declaration of Independence in 1776 — although it is possible that one could have been made in July or August of that year.

5

THE STAR-SPANGLED BANNER

THE THIRTEEN BRITISH COLONIES that created the original United States of America became states in name only on July 4, 1776. They were not officially part of the United States until they ratified the Constitution — three to fourteen years later.

The U.S. government was in its infancy, unsure and just as unorderly. From 1783 to 1785, the capital flag flew in Philadelphia; Princeton, New Jersey; Annapolis, Maryland; Trenton, New Jersey; and New York. From 1786 to 1787, the country was in a severe depression that, in Massachusetts, even led to armed rebellion.

On May 25, 1787, the Constitutional Convention met in Philadelphia and, within four months, had drawn up the Constitution of the United States. It was ratified the following year and put into effect. George Washington took the oath of office as the first president of the United States.

In 1784, an attempt was made by settlers to gain admittance as a state in what is now Tennessee. The federal government ignored the frontier organization's petitions, and after four years the attempt was abandoned.

In 1791, Vermont was admitted to the Union, with Kentucky following in 1792. In 1800, Congress was to adopt a resolution saying that any land acquired by the United States would belong to all and would become a new state, admitted into the Union as an equal.

On December 26, 1793, Stephen Bradley, a senator from Vermont, proposed a bill to alter the national flag. It stated that as of May 1, 1795, the U.S. flag should be 15 stripes of alternate red and white with a union of 15 white stars on a blue field. The Senate passed the bill on December 30, 1795.

The House of Representatives debated the bill. Representative Goodhue of Massachusetts called it "a trifling Business" that would require altering for years. Some members of the House thought the new states should be honored on the flag, while others felt the flag should remain in its original form. Still others, such as Goodhue and Thatcher (also from Massachusetts) felt the entire affair "a consummate piece of frivolity."

An attempt was made to amend the bill, to make the flag permanent and thereby eliminate future changes. This was voted down and the bill in its original form was passed on January 13, 1794, by a vote of 50 to 42. The design was not clarified.

Thus, the Second Flag Act, almost as ambiguous as the first, was enacted. The 15-stripe, 15-star flag remained the national ensign for nearly 25 years — until 1818. Five states were admitted into the Union under the 15-star, 15-stripe flag: Tennessee in 1796, Ohio in 1803, Louisiana in 1812, Indiana in 1816 and Mississippi in 1817. The 15-star, 15-stripe flag was the first flag to fly over the country's new capital, Washington, D.C., on November 17, 1800. After the Louisiana Territory was bought from France, the U.S. flag replaced the French flag in New Orleans on December 20, 1803. Explorers Meriwether Lewis and William Clark carried the 15 stripes and stars across the continent the following year.

30. Original Star-Spangled Banner (1814)

Three warships were also launched under this flag: the *United States*, the *Constellation* and the *Constitution*, making the United States second only to Great Britain as a naval power. The *Constitution* became known as *"Old Ironsides"* when in a battle with the English ship *Guerriere* the cannon balls bounced off her unseasoned oak sides without splintering the timbers. The *Constitution* is now the oldest commissioned warship afloat in any navy. She is presently on the Charles River near Boston, Massachusetts.

In 1805, 15 stripes and stars was raised over the fortress of Derna, in Tripoli, ending the undeclared war with the Barbary pirates in North Africa and becoming the first American flag to fly over any Old World fortress.

During the War of 1812 with England, the U.S. ships flying this flag won a number of victories, bringing to an end the seizures of American ships and the impressment of American seamen into the Royal Navy.

The U.S. Army still did not use a national flag except over its fortresses, and it is the 15 stars and stripes that were flying over Fort McHenry in Baltimore on September 12-14, 1814, that inspired our national anthem.

The writing of America's national anthem and the phrase "star-spangled banner" were directly attributable to a Dr. William Beanes' being confined on board an English ship outside Baltimore. His friends, worried about punishment or deportation, asked a lawyer and friend, Francis Scott Key, to intercede. Key and Colonel J.S. Skinner went aboard the British flagship and, several days and much discussion later, received British Admiral Cochrane's promise to release the doctor. While being entertained aboard the flagship, Key and Skinner inadvertently learned of the coming attack on Baltimore and were forced to remain on a tender until after the battle.

Key and Skinner watched the bombardment of Fort McHenry. During the night of September 13, the cannons stopped firing. Had the fort surrendered?

It had not, and it was the sight of the flag — 42 feet long, 30 feet high, with 15 stars and stripes — that gave the men their answer "by the dawn's early light" as they watched the British leave in defeat.

The sight inspired Key to write the verses later known as America's national anthem. While there are different versions as to how the anthem was written, the version given here was printed in the *Baltimore Patriot* and the *American* (local newspapers) within the week. For unknown reasons, the identity of Key was kept secret for some time by both publications. The tune used for the song was "To Anacreaon in Heaven," a popular English tune and Irish drinking song.

The original star-spangled banner that flew over Fort McHenry is preserved at the Smithsonian Institution in Washington, D.C. It has 11 holes shot through it, but one can still see that the 15 five-pointed stars are arranged in five staggered rows of three each (*Illustration 30*).

A flag of a varying design flew at Stonington, Connecticut, during an attack on August 9-10, 1814. It had 16 stars (arranged in four rows) and 16 stripes. It is presumed this flag was made after the admittance of Tennessee as a state in 1796, but before the admittance of Ohio in 1803. However, the Second Flag Act was still in effect; therefore this was not an official flag (*Illustration 31*).

One other noteworthy flag of this period is the Fort Hill flag, which flew over Fort Hill, Maine, during the War of 1812. The 15 stars and 15 stripes are not arranged in any particular order. The Fort Hill flag is on display in the Smithsonian Institution (*Illustration 32*).

The 15-star and 15-stripe Star-Spangled Banner is the only flag to have a national anthem written for it:

Oh, say can you see by the dawn's early light
What so proudly we hailed at the twilight's last gleaming,
Whose broad stripes and bright stars through the perilous fight,
O'er the ramparts we watch'd, were so gallantly streaming?
And the rockets' red glare, the bombs bursting in air,
Gave proof through the night that our flag was still there;
Oh, say does that star-spangled banner yet wave,
O'er the land of the free, and the home of the brave?

On the shore, dimly seen through the mists of the deep,
Where the foe's haughty host in dread silence reposes,
What is that which the breeze, o'er the towering steep,
As it fitfully blows, half conceals, half discloses?
Now it catches the gleam of the morning's first beam,
In full glory reflected now shines in the stream,
'Tis the star-spangled banner,
Oh, long may it wave,
O'er the land of the free and the home of the brave!

And where is that band who so vauntingly swore
That the havoc of war and battle's confusion,
A home and a country, shall leave us no more?
Their blood has washed out their foul footsteps' pollution.
No refuge could save the hireling and slave,
From the terror of flight or the gloom of the grave,
And the star-spangled banner in triumph doth wave,
O'er the land of the free, and the home of the brave!

Oh, thus be it ever when freemen shall stand,
Between their lov'd home, and the war's desolation!
Blest with vict'ry and peace, may the Heav'n rescued land,
Praise the Power that hath made and preserv'd us a nation.
Then conquer we must, when our cause it is just,
And this be our motto — In God is our Trust;
And the star-spangled banner in triumph shall wave,
O'er the land of the free, and the home of the brave!

31. Stonington, Connecticut, flag (1814)

32. Fort Hill, Maine, flag (1812)

In 1916, President Woodrow Wilson ordered that the "Star-Spangled Banner" be played at all official occasions.

President Herbert Hoover signed the bill designating the "Star-Spangled Banner" as the national anthem on March 3, 1931.

During the playing or singing of the national anthem when the flag is displayed, everyone present (unless in uniform) should stand at attention and face the flag with his right hand over his heart. Men not in uniform should remove their headdress with their right hand and hold it at the left shoulder with their right hand over the heart. Persons in uniform should give the military salute from the first note of the anthem until the last note.

When the flag is not displayed, those present should look toward the music and act as if the flag were before them.

Francis Scott Key's Star-Spangled Banner flies 24 hours a day over both his birthplace and his grave.

PRE-CIVIL WAR OFFICIAL FLAGS

$\star$ 6

AFTER THE WAR OF 1812, it was obvious that the Flag Law of 1795 would have to be amended. The first 15 states each had a star and a stripe in the flag, signifying their being a part of the United States. Since the admission of the 15th state, Kentucky, three more states had been admitted: Tennessee on June 1, 1796; Ohio on March 1, 1803; and Louisiana on April 30, 1812. It was Indiana's turn on December 11, 1816; and Mississippi's on December 10, 1817. That made five states not represented on the national flag.

In 1816, a new congressman from New York, Peter Wendover, had convinced Congress that action was necessary, and he was made chairman of a committee to study the problem. Wendover sought the advice of Samuel Reid, a naval hero of the War of 1812.

Reid suggested reducing the number of stripes to 13 to symbolize the original colonies, and using one additional star for each state admitted into the Union thereafter. The committee presented Reid's suggestions in the form of a recommendation to Congress on January 2, 1817. However, due to a short session, Congress took no action on the recommendation.

On December 17, 1817 (Congress's next session), Wendover again asked for a committee to study the need to change the flag. The same committee was formed again, and it submitted the same recommendations in the form of a bill to the House of Representatives the following January. In March of 1818, Wendover argued the bill on the floor of the House. It was passed on March 25 and signed into law on April 4. The Third Flag Act reads as follows:

> Sect. 1.   Be it enacted…, That from and after the fourth day of July next, the flag of the United States be thirteen horizontal stripes, alternate red and white; that the union have twenty stars, white in a blue field.

Sect. 2.   And be it further enacted, That on the admission of every new State into the Union, one star be added to the union of the flag; and that such addition shall take effect on the fourth of July next succeeding such admission.

As of 1990, 172 years later, the Third Flag Act was still in effect. When comparing it to the first and second flag acts of 1777 and 1794, it is interesting to note that the only actual changes were to set the number of stripes permanently at 13, make the stripes horizontal and fix the number of stars to reflect the number of states in the Union. Because the placement of stars, as well as the overall size of the flag, the stripes, the stars, the canton, and so on, were not mentioned, the design of the flag was still unregulated and left to the individual flagmaker's discretion.

On April 13, 1818, a version of the flag representing the Third Flag Act was raised over the Capitol dome. Sewn by Samuel Reid's wife, it contained 13 horizontal stripes, alternate red and white, and 20 white stars forming one large star in the canton of blue. The flag flew over the Capitol for three months before it was legal on July 4, 1818 (*Illustration 33*).

The U.S. Navy made the first official attempt to standardize the flag on May 18, 1818. It issued a directive, which was amended on September 18, 1818, stating that the stars should be placed in uniform rows. The directive also gave proportions for the flag and the canton.

Later in 1818, President James Monroe ordered that the stars be in four equal, parallel rows of five each (*Illustration 34*). The flag designed and sewn by Mrs. Samuel Reid and flying over Capitol Hill was replaced.

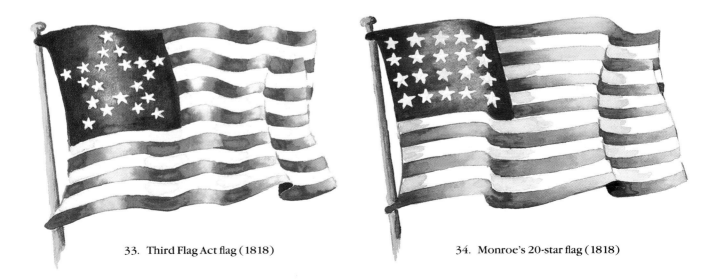

33. Third Flag Act flag (1818)   34. Monroe's 20-star flag (1818)

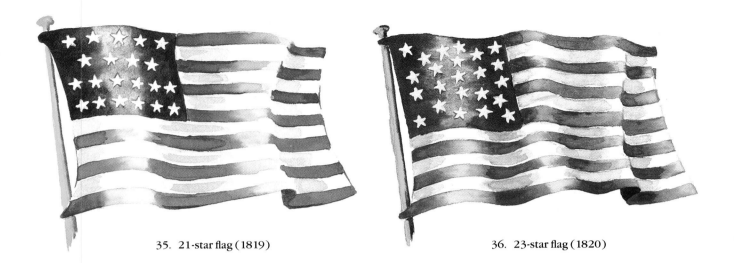

35. 21-star flag (1819)   36. 23-star flag (1820)

The original Stars and Stripes was in use 18 years. The second form of the Stars and Stripes — consisting of 15 stars and 15 stripes — was in use for 23 years. The third flag — 13 stripes and 20 stars — lasted only one year. Illinois became the 21st state to enter the Union in December 1818. The fourth rendition of the Stars and Stripes, with 13 stripes and 21 stars, became the official flag on July 4, 1819 (*Illustration 35*).

Although this flag was officially correct for only one year, it is the first national flag to automatically come into existence with the addition of another state to the Union.

1819 marked the beginning of open disagreement between the North and the South over slavery. Alabama was admitted into the Union on December 14, 1819, becoming the 11th slave state and matching the 11 free states in number. Then Maine began pushing for statehood, which, if granted, would upset the tenuous peace and balance between the North and the South.

In an effort to pacify both sides over the slave issue, a senator from Illinois, Jesse Thomas, made a proposal that would become known as the Missouri Compromise. The Missouri Compromise stated that, with the exception of Missouri, no new slave states could be carved from any lands obtained from the Louisiana Purchase north of the southern boundary of the Missouri Territory. The compromise kept the peace a short while longer.

Congress voted to accept Maine as a free state and Missouri as a slave state as outlined in the Missouri Compromise, but due to problems with Missouri's constitution, only Maine was admitted into the Union in time for the next flag. On March 15, 1820, Maine became the 23rd state. On July 4 of that year, the official flag of the nation became one of 13 stripes and 23 stars (*Illustration 36*).

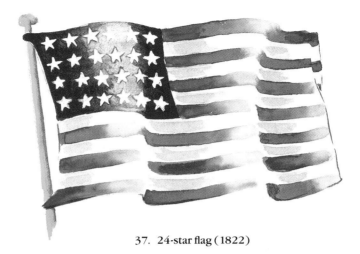

37. 24-star flag (1822)

The 24th star was added on July 4, 1822, after the admission of Missouri into the Union on August 10, 1821. The 24-star flag was in use for 14 years (*Illustration 37*). Three presidents served under this flag: Monroe, John Quincy Adams and Andrew Jackson. During Monroe's lifetime, the Monroe Doctrine was outlined.

The 24-star flag was the original "Old Glory." Captain William Driver received a beautifully made flag from friends in Massachusetts. He hoisted it from his ship, the *Charles Doggett*, saying, "I name her Old Glory." The nickname became widely accepted and is still in use when referring to the American flag. Captain Driver's Old Glory can be seen at the Smithsonian Institution.

In 1830, South Carolina attempted to void federal laws concerning tariffs. This was the first attempt by a state to challenge the central government's power. Had South Carolina succeeded, it might have left the Union. To settle the dispute, Congress passed measures empowering the president to enforce tariffs and diluting the tariffs to a degree that made enforcement unnecessary. Thus ended the first clash over state vs. federal rights requiring congressional intervention.

The U.S. Army officially recognized the flag in 1834, describing it in detail as a garrison flag and allowing it to be carried by troops. The number and name of the regiment it represented were embroidered with gold on the center stripe as stated in Article IV of General Regulations.

In 1836, the Republic of Texas was born, using the Stars and Stripes with one large star in the canton as a naval flag and a large gold star in the center as a national flag. Both were replaced by the "Lone Star" flag in 1839.

During the 24-star flag's reign, anti-slavery forces became a strong power in the political arena. Further steps were taken to keep new slave states from being admitted into the Union. However, Arkansas entered the Union on June 15, 1836, as a slave state, thus creating a new flag on July 4, 1836, consisting of 25 stars (*Illustration 38*).

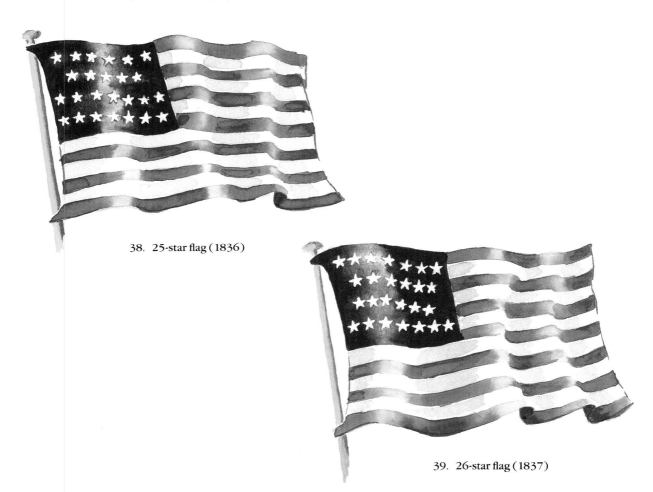

38. 25-star flag (1836)

39. 26-star flag (1837)

Martin Van Buren was elected to the presidency in 1836, becoming the eighth president of the United States but the first president born in the nation he represented. All previous presidents had been born in the New World known as the Americas under the rule of Great Britain. During Van Buren's administration, America suffered its first internally caused, severe depression. Known as the Panic of 1837, it lasted seven hard years.

Michigan became a state on January 26, 1837, giving birth to the 26-star flag on the following Fourth of July (*Illustration 39*). The 26-star flag was officially in existence until 1845. During its eight-year life, President William

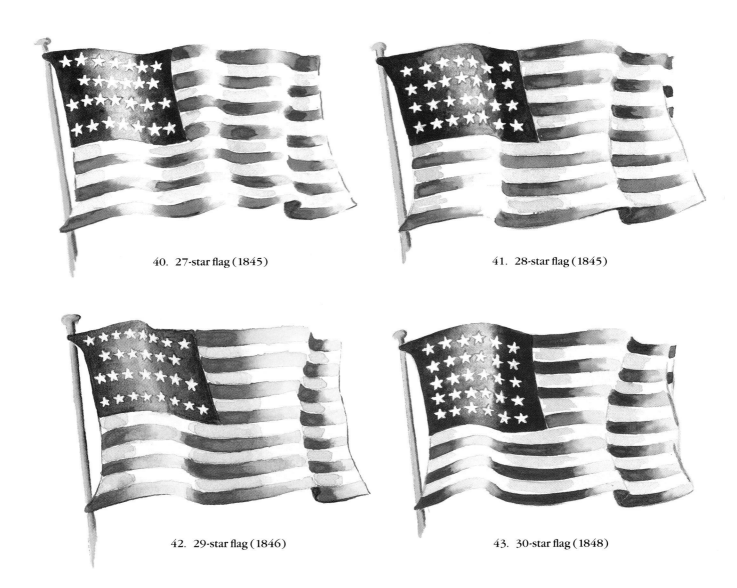

40. 27-star flag (1845)

41. 28-star flag (1845)

42. 29-star flag (1846)

43. 30-star flag (1848)

Henry Harrison became the first president to die in office. John Tyler then became the first vice president promoted to the presidency because of a president's death.

James Polk was elected president in 1844, and during his administration, four new states — and flags — became part of the Union: Florida on March 3, 1845 (*Illustration 40*); Texas on December 29, 1845 (*Illustration 41*); Iowa on December 26, 1846 (*Illustration 42*); and Wisconsin on May 29, 1848 (*Illustration 43*).

It was not illegal to carry or display a variation of the national flag, and many renditions could be seen across the nation. A unique Stars and Stripes flag was carried by General John Fremont during the 1840s while he was charting what was to become the western United States. Known as the "Pathfinder of the West," Fremont carried a personalized flag containing 26 stars in two curved lines of 13 each, with an eagle clutching a bundle of arrows and a peace pipe between the lines of stars (*Illustration 44*).

44. Fremont flag (1840s)

By 1846, the national flag consisted of 28 stars. That year, the United States went to war against Mexico, and from May 13 through February 2, 1848, the army officially carried the Stars and Stripes into battle on land for the first time. However, because the Mexican War was already into its second month when the 28-star flag became official on July 4, 1846, the majority of flags used by the U.S. Army during the war were the 27-star flags.

Also in 1846, California declared itself an independent republic, and Iowa was admitted into the Union on December 26. The 28-star flag was officially replaced by 29 stars on July 4, 1847. This period saw the end of the Mexican War, the acquisition of New Mexico and California for $15 million, and the establishment of the Rio Grande as the official boundary between Mexico and this country (Treaty of Guadalupe Hidalgo).

On May 29, 1848, Wisconsin entered the Union. The 12th design of the U.S. flag (30 stars) was used during the administrations of President James Polk, Zachary Taylor and Millard Fillmore.

45. 31-star flag (1851)

California became a state on September 9, 1850. The flag grew to 31 stars the following July (*Illustration 45*). It was used during the remainder of Fillmore's term of office and saw two more presidents elected: Franklin Pierce and James Buchanan. Commodore Oliver Perry carried the 31-star flag, making it the first American flag to be displayed in Japan (1853).

July 4, 1858, boosted the star count to 32 with the admittance of Minnesota as a state on May 11, 1858, under the Buchanan administration (*Illustration 46*). Oregon became a state on February 14, 1859. On July 4, 1860, the American flag consisted of 33 stars (*Illustration 47*).

46. 32-star flag (1858)

47. 33-star flag (1860)

The anti-slavery issue continued to gain momentum. Less than two years after the official birth of the 33-star flag, 11 of the 33 states represented in the official flag had seceded from the Union, beginning with South Carolina on December 28, 1860, and followed by Mississippi, Florida, Alabama, Georgia, Louisiana and Texas within the next six weeks. Historians tell us the deciding factor for the withdrawal of these states was the election of Abraham Lincoln as the 16th President. The Confederate States of America, complete with a national flag, was formed.

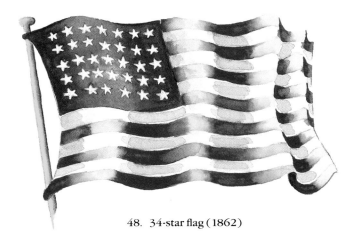

48. 34-star flag (1862)

While the original seven Confederate states were separating from the Union, Kansas was attempting to enter as the 34th state. After much bickering among residents, a constitution that legalized slavery was drawn up and submitted to a popular vote — twice. The first vote upheld the original constitution allowing slavery. A second vote defeated the same constitution. In 1858, President Buchanan, ignoring the second vote, recommended Kansas be admitted as a slave state. Congress insisted the constitution be resubmitted to the people for yet another vote. Once again, the constitution was rejected by the people of Kansas, and in 1859, a new constitution was drawn up. It prohibited slavery and was ratified by the citizens. Kansas entered the Union as a free state on January 29, 1861, becoming the 34th *official* state and automatically creating the corresponding official flag on the following Fourth of July (*Illustration 48*). Needless to say, the 34-star flag was not recognized by the seceding states as their official flag.

FORD'S THEATRE

BENEFIT!

LAST NIGHT

LAURA KEENE

CIVIL WAR FLAGS

THE CONFEDERATE STATES flew many different flags, none of which was recognized by the government of the United States. Georgia, Virginia and North Carolina used flags patterned after their state flags. Louisiana used a flag with a pelican on it but changed to 13 red, white and blue stripes with a lone yellow star in a red canton. The flag consisting of a blue field with a large white star and known as the "Bonnie Blue" flag was one of the more popular flags to represent a united cause over the entire South (*Illustration 49*).

On March 4, 1861, a committee voted to accept, as a flag representing the Confederate States of America, one consisting of a red field with a white space running horizontally through the center and one-third of its width. The red spaces above and below were the same size as the white with a blue canton down to the lower red stripe and a circle of white stars representing each state of the Confederacy inside the canton. The flag became known as the Stars and Bars (*Illustration 50*).

President Lincoln took office in March 1861. On the dawn of April 12, 1861, the Confederacy opened fire on Fort Sumter, South Carolina. Two days later, Major Anderson of the U.S. Army surrendered, and the Stars and Stripes was struck.

In May and June 1861, four more states withdrew from the Union and joined the Confederacy: Virginia, Arkansas, Tennessee, and North Carolina. There were now 11 Confederate states.

Rising hatred between free states and seceding slave states saw a movement by staunch Unionists to remove a star for each withdrawing state from the national flag. Some extremists even went so far as to make flags with 23 stars, but these flags were unauthorized by the U.S. government.

The Stars and Stripes' 34-star flag went into battle against the Stars and Bars on July 21, 1861, at Bull Run, Virginia. The Confederates discovered that their flag was too similar to the Union flag in the confusion of battle, so another flag was created for battle use. Square in shape, it had a red field with a blue diagonal cross encompassing 13 white stars across the field. Sometimes

49. Bonnie Blue flag

50. Confederate Stars and Bars flag (1861)

51. Rebel flag/Southern Cross

52. 35-star flag (1863)

the blue was also outlined in white. This new battle flag was referred to as the Rebel flag or the Southern Cross and became extremely popular throughout the Confederacy (*Illustration 51*). However, in spite of its widespread popularity, the battle flag was never officially adopted by the Confederate States of America.

In 1861, the northwestern counties of Virginia, in a revolt against the rest of the state, refused to recognize the secession of Virginia. They organized a separate Unionist government with a constitution providing for a gradual freeing of slaves. When admitted into the Union on June 20, 1863, West Virginia obtained the distinction of becoming not only the 35th state, but also the only state in America's history to be formed from an existing state without the original state's consent.

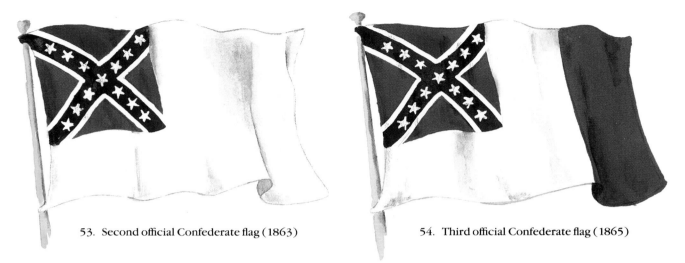

53. Second official Confederate flag (1863)   54. Third official Confederate flag (1865)

On July 4, 1863, the 35th star, representing West Virginia, was officially added to the Stars and Stripes (*Illustration 52*). During the same year, the Confederate states also altered their flag from the Stars and Bars to one consisting of a white field with the red Battle Flag in its canton (*Illustration 53*).

Neither change was noticed to much degree. The 35-star flag was never issued to Union troops. The new Confederate flag was never accepted by the Confederate soldiers over their popular battle flag, the Southern Cross. In addition, it was felt that the new Confederate flag, with its white field, too closely resembled a truce or surrender flag. Therefore, the 35-star Stars and Stripes and the Southern Cross (or Rebel flag) continued to represent the North and the South in their struggle on land. The new flags were used mainly aboard ships.

On March 4, 1865, President Jefferson Davis of the Confederate states approved an act revising the previous Confederate flag. A vertical red bar was added at the end of the white field opposite the union (*Illustration 54*).

Less than a month later (April 9, 1865), General Robert E. Lee surrendered, bringing an official end to the bloodiest war in the history of the United States. Unofficial skirmishes between the North and the South continued until May or June of 1865. The total cost in lives has been estimated at between 600,000 and 800,000.

Five days after Lee's surrender, Lincoln was dead from a gunshot wound, the result of an assassination as he attended a play at Ford's Theater in Washington, D.C. He was the first U.S. president to be killed in office.

It was not until 1865 that Tennessee would be officially readmitted into the Union with full rights. The remaining 10 Confederate states were readmitted with full rights between 1868 and 1870. After the last state was readmitted, all federal occupation troops were recalled by the U.S. government, and the reunited country began the slow healing from the ravages of war.

NORTH
POLE

CIVIL WAR TO PRESENT ★ 8

Nevada was recognized as a territory in 1861. Between that time and its admittance into the Union in 1864, Congress was trying to ratify the Constitution in order to outlaw slavery. Nevada's population was less than 20 percent of the required number of 127,381 needed to become a state. However, President Lincoln needed Nevada as a state to support his anti-slavery amendments. An agreement was struck whereby the population requirement was waived in exchange for Nevada's promise to vote for the proposal against slavery slated to be put before Congress. Nevada was admitted into the Union on October 31, 1864, becoming the 36th *official* state and officially revising the star count of the Stars and Stripes to 36 on July 4, 1865 (*Illustration 55*).

The proposal to legally abolish slavery was presented in Congress on January 31, 1865. On December 6, 1865, the bill was passed into law, making it the 13th amendment to the Constitution of the United States.

Nebraska became a territory in 1854, winning approval for statehood from Congress in 1864. By 1866, Nebraska residents had ratified their state's constitution in accordance with the federal Constitution and the state was admitted into the Union on March 1, 1867. That brought the star count of the official Stars and Stripes to 37 the following July 4 (*Illustration 56*).

The 19th official flag design was in effect from July 4, 1867, through July 3, 1877. It flew during the terms of three presidents: Andrew Johnson, Ulysses S. Grant and Rutherford B. Hayes.

One hundred years after the birth of the United States, Colorado (the Centennial State) joined the Union on August 1, 1876. The 38-star flag, also known as the Centennial flag, served its country from July 4, 1877, until July 3, 1890 (*Illustration 57*). During its 13-year history, James Garfield was elected president in 1881, only to be shot down four months after taking office by a disappointed citizen seeking a government position. He died of his wounds six months later, the second president assassinated in office. Vice President Chester Arthur assumed the role of president for the balance of the term. In

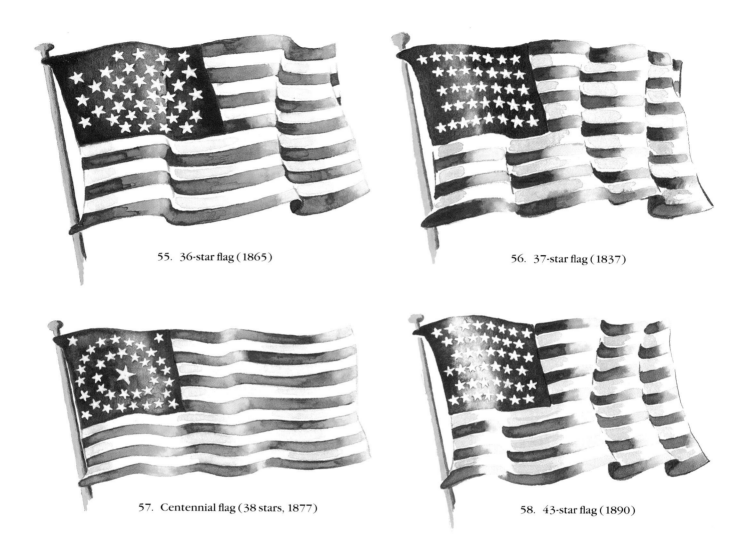

55. 36-star flag (1865)

56. 37-star flag (1837)

57. Centennial flag (38 stars, 1877)

58. 43-star flag (1890)

1884, Grover Cleveland was elected president. He was succeeded by Benjamin Harrison.

During November of 1889, North Dakota, South Dakota, Montana and Washington were admitted into the Union. Idaho joined on July 3, 1890. The official flag of July 4, 1890, jumped from 38 stars to 43 stars (*Illustration 58*). However, because Idaho joined the Union one day before stars were officially added to the national flag, the majority of the flags made for the period from July 4, 1890, through July 3, 1891, displayed 42 stars — an unofficial rendition of the U.S. flag.

Wyoming was admitted into the Union on July 10, 1890, seven days after Idaho but six days too late to be included in the official flag of that year. On July 4, 1891, the official flag bore 44 stars (*Illustration 59*).

Utah became the 45th state to join the Union on January 4, 1896. The 23rd rendition of the official flag, 45 stars, saw the end of an economic depression that had gripped the nation since shortly after the inauguration of President Grover Cleveland in March 1893 (*Illustration 60*). The United States now entered a period of economic prosperity.

On February 15, 1898, an American battleship, the *Maine*, was sunk in Havana, Cuba, involving the United States of America in another military conflict. The Spanish-American War was formally declared by Congress on April 21, 1898. The 45-star flag went into a war that was to last 114 days.

President William McKinley was assassinated by an anarchist and died of his gunshot wound on September 14, 1901, the third president to be killed in office. Vice President Theodore Roosevelt, Spanish-American War hero, became the 25th president.

On February 20, 1905, Congress passed the first federal law regarding flag protocol. It provided that no trademark could be registered if it

> consists of or comprises the Flag or coat of arms or other insignia of the United States or any simulation thereof, or of any State or municipality or of any foreign nation.

In 1906, the 45-star flag accompanied Roosevelt, who became the first president to travel beyond the national limits of the United States when he visited Panama and Puerto Rico aboard the battleship *Louisiana*.

Oklahoma became the 46th state on November 16, 1907. The 46-star flag flew from July 4, 1908, through July 3, 1912 (*Illustration 61*). During this period, Admiral Robert E. Peary and his men reached the North Pole. After more than 200 years of unsuccessful attempts by various expeditions, Peary sent a message on April 6, 1909, that reverberated around the world — "Stars and Stripes nailed to the North Pole."

59. 44-star flag (1891)   60. 45-star flag (1896)

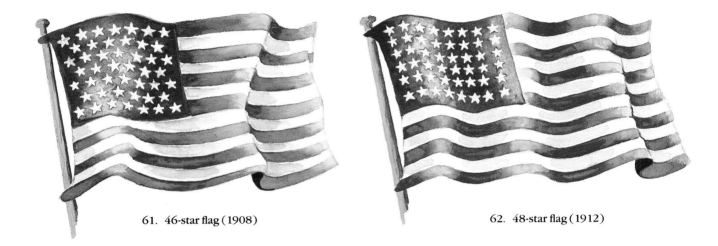

61. 46-star flag (1908)

62. 48-star flag (1912)

A territory since 1850, New Mexico was admitted into the Union on January 6, 1912, as the 47th state. Arizona followed on February 14, 1912. On July 4, 1912, the official national flag consisted of 13 stripes and 48 stars (*Illustration 62*).

While the 48-star flag was in effect, President William Howard Taft (sworn into office in 1909) became the president credited with making the largest contribution to the American flag. A survey made during 1912 revealed that government agencies were using flags of 66 different sizes, most with varying proportions. Nongovernmental flags were even more widespread in their irregularities. To establish some uniformity to the national emblem, Taft issued executive orders on June 24 and October 29 of 1912. They were directed toward all governmental flags and allowed only 12 sizes. In addition, flag proportions were set down as law. The proportions are:

Hoist (height) of flag — 1 unit
Fly (length) of flag — 1.9 units
Hoist of canton — $\frac{7}{13}$ total height
Fly of canton — 0.76 unit
Width of each stripe — $\frac{1}{13}$ total height
Diameter of each star — 0.0616 unit

The 48-star flag was in effect longer than any other U.S. flag. Eight presidents served during its 47 years: William Howard Taft, Woodrow Wilson, Warren G. Harding, Calvin Coolidge, Herbert C. Hoover, Franklin D. Roosevelt (the second president to die of natural causes while in office), Harry S. Truman and Dwight D. Eisenhower.

The United States entered World War I under the 48-star flag on April 6, 1917. Under President Wilson, the U.S. joined forces with Great Britain, France,

Russia, Belgium, Italy, Japan and other allies against Germany, Austria-Hungary, Turkey and Bulgaria. The war ended on November 11, 1918.

The forerunner of the United Nations, the League of Nations, was formed at the Paris Peace Conference in 1919. It consisted of 26 nations, including the United States. However, Congress did not ratify its membership, and the organization was weakened dramatically for this reason.

For 20 years after World War I, the 48-star flag flew over a nation at peace with the world if not with itself. It waved during the Roaring Twenties and Prohibition. It endured the Great Depression of the thirties.

1941 saw the Stars and Stripes entering World War II, bringing to an end both peace and the depression. Along with Great Britain, France, the Soviet Union and other allies, the United States fought Germany, Italy and Japan. Once more, the 48-star flag flew triumphant at the war's end, on September 2, 1945.

The Stars and Stripes became an integral part of a monument to the American men and women who died during World War II, the Iwo Jima Memorial near Washington, D.C. The bronze statue was based upon a photograph taken by U.S. war correspondent Joe Rosenthal. It shows five Marines and one sailor raising the U.S. flag atop Mount Suribachi within an hour after winning a battle that had cost nearly 6,000 American lives. An actual American flag is incorporated into the statue and flies day and night by executive order. The Iwo Jima Memorial can be viewed at Arlington National Cemetery.

The United Nations was formed on October 24, 1945, in New York City. Fifty-one independent countries banded together to promote peace and international security in a cooperative effort to banish war from the face of Earth.

In 1949, 14 countries formed the North Atlantic Treaty Organization (NATO) to implement the North Atlantic Treaty of 1949. Its purpose was to counterweigh the Soviet military presence in Europe.

But despite these peace efforts, the following year found the 48-star flag accompanying its armed forces into battle again. The United States, in compliance with the provisions set forth by the United Nations, entered the Korean conflict, a military action between North and South Korea. Within one hour of the successful American amphibious landing at Inchon, the American flag was raised. The undeclared war lasted three years before the American flag returned home, neither triumphant or defeated, to peace once more.

On September 8, 1954, the 48-star flag was witness to yet another organization formed in the hopes of ensuring world peace. The United States, Great Britain, France, New Zealand, Australia, the Philippines, Thailand and Pakistan formed the Southeast Asia Treaty Organization (SEATO) for mutual defense — an agreement that some historians maintain ensured the involvement of the United States in Vietnam some 10 years later.

The 48-star flag flew into space in 1958. The United States joined Russia in the space race on January 31, with the first successful launch of the satellite *Explorer I* from Cape Canaveral, Florida. On July 29, 1958, the National Aeronautics and Space Administration (NASA) was established to provide civilian control and coordination of space exploration.

After 47 years as a territory, Alaska was approved for admittance into the Union by Congress on June 30, 1958. It became the 49th state on January 3, 1959, bringing the official national flag's star count to 49 on July 4, 1959 (*Illustration 63*). Purchased from Russia in 1867, Alaska was the first state outside the contiguous boundaries of the United States. It is twice the size of Texas, and it contains the highest mountain in the United States, Mt. McKinley (20,300 feet). The 49-star flag officially flew for one year.

The United States officially recognized its next state, Hawaii, for the first time on August 7, 1894. During the Spanish-American War of 1898, the value of the Hawaiian Islands as a naval base became apparent. Pressure for annexation was increased. In 1900 Hawaii became a U.S. territory. It was approved for statehood by Congress on March 18, 1959. Hawaiians voted to become the 50th state on June 27 of that year and officially entered the Union on August 21. The territorial flag of Hawaii, made up of eight red, white and blue stripes with a British Union in the canton, was replaced by the 50-star Stars and Stripes on July 4, 1960.

The 50-star rendition of the Stars and Stripes (*Illustration 64*) became the first to fly over soil other than Earth's when, on July 20, 1969, astronauts Neil Armstrong and Edwin Aldrin placed it on the moon.

On November 22, 1963, the 50-star flag flew at half-mast throughout the country and the world as the United States' youngest president, John F. Kennedy, became the fourth president in American history to be assassinated. Vice President Lyndon B. Johnson succeeded to office.

In 1964, Congress passed a law defining the misuse of the Stars and Stripes and the punishment for those found guilty:

> Whoever knowingly casts contempt upon any flag of the United States by publicly mutilating, defacing, defiling, burning, or trampling upon it shall be fined not more than $1,000 or imprisoned for not more than one year, or both.

The 50-star flag became the first U.S. flag to become part of a dispute between the United States and another country over its display. From January 9-17, 1964, riots erupted in the Panama Canal Zone because the Stars and Stripes was flown over a high school for American dependents in Panama. The Panamanians felt this action was in direct violation of a previous agreement that neither country's flag would be displayed. Four U.S. soldiers and 21 Panamanians were killed in the riots, and Panama broke diplomatic relations with the U.S. government on January 17, 1964.

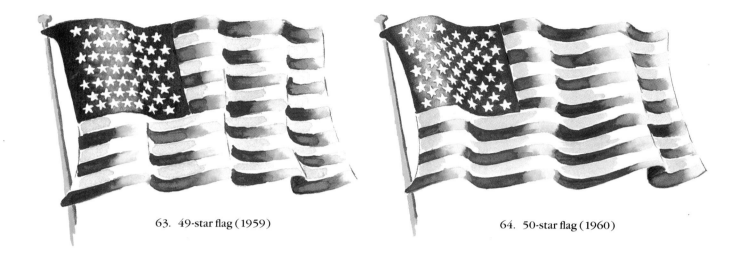

63. 49-star flag (1959)   64. 50-star flag (1960)

On March 8, 1965, U.S. troops first carried the 50-star flag into Vietnam in what was to become America's most unpopular war.

Civil rights leader Martin Luther King, Jr., was shot and killed in Memphis, Tennessee, on April 4, 1968, adding more fuel to the race riots ravaging the country. Senator Robert Kennedy was shot in Los Angeles on June 5, 1968, and died of his wounds 25 hours later. Unrest, bloodshed and protests concerning the U.S. involvement in Vietnam continued to plague the government. The Watergate affair became public knowledge in mid-1972.

"Peace with honor" was achieved on January 23, 1973, bringing an official end to U.S. involvement in the Vietnam War. The flag and the soldiers who fought under it returned home to a country filled with bitterness and suspicion of its government.

The ever-increasing repercussions of Watergate found Vice President Spiro T. Agnew pleading "no contest" to income tax evasion. He resigned his office on October 10, 1973.

Gerald R. Ford was sworn in on December 6, 1973, to serve as vice president under President Richard M. Nixon — the first official to enter office under the provisions of the 25th Amendment of the Constitution of the United States.

Eight months later, Nixon resigned as president, becoming the first president to abdicate. Vice President Gerald Ford was sworn in as president. He was defeated in the presidential election of 1976 by Jimmy Carter.

In 1980, Ronald Reagan was voted into office as the 40th president of the United States. He survived an assassination attempt on March 30, 1981. He recovered from his wounds within a month and was re-elected in 1984. Reagan was succeeded by the man who had served as his vice president, George Bush, in 1988.

HONORING THE STARS AND STRIPES

RESPECT FOR THE FLAG that represents their nation has been shown by patriotic citizens throughout history. The forerunners of the first official flag of the United States were respected by the colonists as emblems of their struggle for freedom. Immense pride and care were given to the official flags born of the first Flag Resolution of June 14, 1777. Americans traditionally celebrate this resolution by observing June 14 of each year as Flag Day.

A surge of patriotism during the early days of the Civil War led to the first recorded observance of Flag Day on June 14, 1861, in Hartford, Connecticut. The first nationwide observance of Flag Day was not until June 14, 1877, the centennial of the original Flag Resolution. However, this nationwide celebration was just held to mark the centennial of the American flag and was not intended to be an annual occurrence.

Twelve years later, in 1889, a kindergarten class at a New York public school held a patriotic exercise commemorating the origin of the national flag. On June 14, 1893, Philadelphia flew flags from public buildings in observance of Flag Day.

In 1916, President Woodrow Wilson issued a proclamation setting aside June 14 as a day to honor the birth of the national flag. In 1926, President Calvin Coolidge issued a similar proclamation.

Pennsylvania is credited with being the first state to establish Flag Day as a legal day of observance. The state law was passed May 7, 1937.

It was not until August 3, 1949, that Congress, in a joint resolution, stated that June 14 of each year be designated as Flag Day. President Harry Truman signed the resolution the same day, thereby making it a national day of legal observance.

Meanwhile, the first flag salute statute had been passed by the New York legislature on April 22, 1898:

> It shall be the duty of the state superintendent of public instruction to prepare, for the use of the public schools of the state, a program providing for a salute to the flag at the opening of each day of school.

The Pledge of Allegiance to the flag is another patriotic custom. During the late 1800s there was a popular children's publication called *Youth's Companion*. James B. Upham, head of its circulation department, was a staunch patriot. He felt that patriotism was waning and began a crusade to revive "old-fashioned" patriotism in the children of America. Through *Youth's Companion*, he proposed that children, to show love for their country and flag, raise funds to buy flags to fly over their schools. The plan was enthusiastically received by adults and children alike. The following year found about 30,000 Stars and Stripes flying over schools from coast to coast.

Upham also felt a need for a strong, vibrant pledge that the children could recite when the flag was raised each morning. The only pledge used to any extent was, "I give my hand and heart to my country, one nation, one language, one flag."

Enlisting the aid of a fellow staff member of *Youth's Companion*, Francis Bellamy, Upham worked on a pledge to be published in the September 8, 1892, issue for the Columbus Day celebration in October. At the same time their proposed pledge was published in *Youth's Companion*, leaflets were sent to schools throughout the country. During the Columbus Day celebration, more than 12 million school children recited Upham's and Bellamy's new pledge:

> I pledge allegiance to my flag and to the Republic for which it stands — one Nation indivisible, with liberty and justice for all.

The pledge printed in *Youth's Companion* was made part of a law passed by the Washington state legislature in 1919. The law said:

> Every board of directors...shall cause appropriate flag exercises to be held in every school at least once in each week at which exercises the pupils shall recite the following salute to the flag: (Upham/Bellamy pledge).

In 1939, a committee was appointed for historical purposes to determine the true authorship of the pledge. Evidence was reviewed by two historians and a political scientist. On May 18, 1939, their unanimous decision gave credit for penning the "Pledge of Allegiance" to Francis Bellamy. While this finding was widely accepted, some contend history shows Upham to be the author. Bellamy did state that he had written the final pledge, but he gave much credit to "that rare and self-retiring patriot, James B. Upham."

The original wording of the Pledge of Allegiance came under criticism because it was felt that immigrants to the United States could be mentally swearing allegiance to their original country. The first National Flag Conference was formed, and on June 14, 1923, its members adopted a change. The words "my flag" were replaced with "the flag of the United States of America." The revised pledge was adopted by Congress as part of the National Flag Code in 1942.

On June 14, 1954, the words "under God" were added by Congress, bringing the Pledge of Allegiance to its current form:

> I pledge allegiance to the Flag of the United States of America and to the Republic for which it stands, one Nation under God, indivisible, with liberty and justice for all.

CONSTITUTIONAL RIGHT OR DISRESPECT?

★10

THROUGHOUT THE HISTORY of the United States, much homage has been given to the Stars and Stripes as a patriotic symbol of freedom. As of 1990, 48 states and the U.S. government had laws against disrespect and/or desecration of the American flag.

However, as early as 1918, religious opposition to the homage shown to the flag, particularly the saluting of the flag, began to appear in the courts. Ora Troyer, a Mennonite of West Liberty, Ohio, was prosecuted for failing to keep his daughter in school. He had instructed her not to participate in the flag salute ceremony, which caused her expulsion. Troyer was convicted and fined in the local court. When he appealed to the Logan County Court of Common Pleas, the judge ruled for the local court and admonished Troyer strongly:

> The child was told by defendant below not to salute.... Such conduct on the part of our citizens is not conscionable...but rather it is the forerunner of disloyalty and treason.

On September 8, 1925, a Mr. and Mrs. Tremain withdrew their 9-year-old son from school, maintaining that his forced participation in the flag exercises violated their religion. Eight days later, Tremain was arrested for contributing to the delinquency of his son. He was convicted and sentenced to eight days in jail. While he was in jail, his son was taken from his home and placed first in a detention home and later in the State Children's Home. The child was made a ward of the court on June 4, 1926, and put up for adoption.

The American Civil Liberties Union tried to pursue the matter but was unable to get into court. The child was returned to his parents on November 28, 1927, on the condition he be placed in a public or private school.

In 1928, 38 Mennonite children were expelled from the Greenwood, Delaware, public schools for refusing to salute the flag. Once again, the American Civil Liberties Union offered to represent the children on the grounds of constitutional infringement, but the Mennonites' doctrine of nonresistance would not allow it.

Minersville, Pennsylvania, schools had an established flag salute custom since 1914. Early in October 1935, Lillian Gobitis (seventh grade) and her brother, William (fifth grade), refused to participate in the flag ceremony because of their religion (Jehovah's Witness). On October 21, 1935, Edmund Wasliewski (sixth grade), also refused to salute the flag. On November 6, 1935, all three students were expelled. Mr. Gobitis tried to enroll his children in Pottsville, Pennsylvania, but because the same customs were practiced in Pottsville, his attempt failed.

On March 3, 1937, Gobitis filed a bill of complaint in the U.S. District Court for Eastern District of Pennsylvania, stating his constitutional rights under the Eighth and Fourteenth Amendments had been violated. The trial was held in the District Court on February 15, 1938. A decision against the Minersville school board was handed down on November 9, 1938. The school board appealed to the U.S. Supreme Court, which on June 3, 1940, overturned the lower court's decision and held that public school authorities could constitutionally expel a child for refusing on religious grounds to salute the American flag.

The same court overruled its previous holding in the West Virginia State Board of Education vs. Barnette case on June 14, 1943 (Flag Day). It ruled that no civilian, adult or child, could be compelled to salute the flag, nor be subjected to disabilities for refusing to do so, whatever his reason for refusing.

During the 1960s it became increasingly popular to wear a rendition of the American flag on one's clothing and use it in other decorative ways. Although the Flag Code specifically states that

> [the] flag should never be used as a wearing apparel, bedding or drapery...not be embroidered on such articles as cushions or handkerchiefs and the like...no part of the flag should ever be used as a costume...,

the code is not law. Individual states and the U.S. government have laws protecting the flag against defilement and/or disrespect. However, as with the laws concerning saluting the flag, interpretation and intent must be taken into consideration to make sure that an individual's constitutional rights are not violated.

On January 31, 1970, a complaint was sworn out by a Leominster, Massachusetts, police officer against a Mr. Goguen under the contempt provision of the Massachusetts flag-misuse statute. The complaint stated Goguen "did publicly treat contemptuously the flag of the United States." Goguen had been seen the previous day wearing an American flag about 4 by 6 inches on the left rear seat of his blue jeans. A jury trial was held in the Worcester County Superior Court, where Goguen was found guilty and sentenced to six months in the Massachusetts House of Corrections.

Goguen appealed to the Massachusetts Supreme Judicial Court, which affirmed his sentence. He was later granted bail and ordered released on a writ of *habeas corpus* by the U.S. District Court for the District of Massachusetts. The court found the flag contempt portion of the statute vague under the due process clause of the Fourteenth Amendment and overbroad under the First Amendment. The conviction was overturned.

The U.S. Constitution, particularly the First and Fourteenth Amendments, guarantees its citizens the right to express their beliefs.

Gregory Lee Johnson, a member of the Revolutionary Communist Youth Brigade, traveled to Dallas, Texas, to protest Reagan administration policies during the 1984 Republican National Convention. Johnson, in front of Dallas City Hall, doused an American flag with lighter fluid and set it on fire. He and fellow protesters chanted, "America, the red, white and blue, we spit on you" as the 50-star flag burned on the sidewalk.

Johnson was charged with violation of the Texas Penal Code, which reads in part:

> A person commits an offense if he intentionally or knowingly desecrates…a state or national flag…. For purposes of this section, "desecrate" means deface, damage or otherwise physically mistreat in a way that the actor knows will seriously offend one or more persons likely to observe or discover his action.

Found guilty, Johnson was sentenced to one year in prison and fined $2,000. The conviction was upheld by the Court of Appeals but was reversed by the Texas Court of Criminal Appeals, which maintained that the conviction was in direct conflict of Johnson's constitutional rights under the First Amendment. The U.S. Supreme Court, in a 5—4 ruling, upheld the Texas Court of Criminal Appeals. The last sentence in the high court ruling stated:

Moreover, this Court will not create an exception to these principles protected by the First Amendment for the American flag alone.

Controversy resounded across the nation. President George Bush said burning the flag was "wrong, dead wrong." The Senate passed a resolution expressing "profound disappointment." Yet Justice William Brennan, who delivered the opinion of the court, wrote:

We do not consecrate the flag by punishing its desecration, for in doing so we dilute the freedom that this cherished emblem represents.

The First Amendment of the Constitution, ratified on December 15, 1791, reads:

Congress shall make no law respecting an establishment of religion, or prohibiting the free exercise thereof; or abridging the freedom of speech, or of the press; or the right of the people peaceably to assemble, and to petition the Government for a redress of grievances.

Section One of the Fourteenth Amendment reads:

All persons born or naturalized in the United States, and subject to the jurisdiction thereof, are citizens of the United States and of the State wherein they reside. No State shall make or enforce any law which shall abridge the privileges or immunities of citizens of the United States; nor shall any State deprive any person of life, liberty, or property, without due process of law; nor deny to any person within its jurisdiction the equal protection of the laws.

Historical Dates Pertaining to the Flag and Its Country

June 17, 1775	Flags representing colonists in their fight for freedom appear in battle for the first time against the British at Breed's Hill and Bunker Hill near Boston. These flags are of various designs and colors with little, if any, resemblance to the Stars and Stripes of later years. A vast majority of the flags carry a pine tree in the field of the flag.
November 29, 1775	Captain John Manley, commander of the U.S. naval vessel *Lee* captures the British brigantine *Nancy*, striking the British colors and replacing it with a green and white flag including a pine tree emblem.
January 1, 1776	The Grand Union flag, the first common national flag, is raised over Prospect Hill in Boston at General Washington's headquarters during the forming of the Continental Army. Basically a British Meteor flag, it has six horizontal white stripes added across the red field. It is not an official national flag.
March 1776	The Grand Union flag goes to sea for the first time as the flag representing the new Continental Navy.
June 14, 1777	The First Flag Law is passed by Congress, giving this country an official national flag. The flag is to consist of 13 stripes, alternate red and white, and a union consisting of 13 white stars on a blue field.
August 16, 1777	A version of the Stars and Stripes is flown in a land battle for the first time at the Battle of Bennington on the New York–Vermont border. Dubbed the Bennington flag, it is the oldest known Stars and Stripes flag in existence.

November 1, 1777	The first use of the Stars and Stripes at sea is documented when Captain John Paul Jones hoists the flag on the *Ranger*, a U.S. warship, before sailing out of Portsmouth, New Hampshire.
January 28, 1778	The Stars and Stripes is raised over foreign soil for the first time when ships of the U.S. Navy capture Fort Nassau in the Bahama Islands.
February 14, 1778	The Stars and Stripes receives its first offiicial recognition in a foreign port when it is rendered a nine-gun salute from the French at Quiberon Bay near Brest, France. The ship is under the command of John Paul Jones.
February 4, 1783	The Revolutionary War ends and the Stars and Stripes is recognized by the world as the national flag of a new nation, the United States of America.
August 1790	The Stars and Stripes completes its first trip around the world aboard the *Columbia* under the command of Captain Robert Gray. It had left Boston on September 30, 1787, and traveled 42,000 miles before its return to Boston.
May 1, 1795	Congress passes the Second Flag Law, adding two stripes and stars to the national flag in recognition of Vermont and Kentucky. The 15-striped, 15-star flag is the second official version of the national flag.
November 17, 1800	The Stars and Stripes is hoisted over the Capitol in the sixth, and present, U.S. capital, Washington, D.C.
December 20, 1803	The Stars and Stripes replaces the French flag over New Orleans after completion of the Louisiana Purchase, the first major land acquisition of the United States.
1804	The American flag makes its first complete crossing of the continent when it is carried to the Pacific by the Lewis and Clark expedition.
April 27, 1805	The Stars and Stripes flies over an Old World fortress for the first time, bringing to an end the undeclared war with the Barbary pirates of Derna, Tripoli, in North Africa.
September 20, 1814	The "Star-Spangled Banner" is first published as a poem in the *Baltimore Patriot* newspaper. Francis Scott Key composed the verses in honor of the defense of Fort McHenry during the War of 1812. It is subsequently put to music and, on March 3, 1931, becomes the national anthem.
April 4, 1818	Congress passes the Third Flag Act, creating the third official version of the Stars and Stripes. The national flag reverts back to 13 stripes to symbolize the original colonies. It is decided that a star for each state admitted to the Union should be automatically added to the union of the flag on the Fourth of July after each admittance. The third Stars and Stripes consists of 13 stripes and 20 stars.

July 4, 1819	The first star is automatically added to the flag in accordance with the Flag Law of the previous year. It recognizes the admission of Illinois into the Union and becomes the fourth official design of the Stars and Stripes.
July 4, 1820	The fifth official design of the Stars and Stripes is created with stars added for Alabama and Maine, for a total of 23 stars.
July 4, 1822	The sixth official national flag is created with the admission of the 24th state, Missouri.
March 17, 1824	The Stars and Stripes becomes known as "Old Glory" after Captain William Driver hoists a new 24-star flag from his ship, the *Charles Doggett*. The flag was a gift to the captain.
1834	The national flag is authorized by the U.S. Army as a regimental color, the first official field use of the American flag by a military unit.
July 4, 1836	The seventh official design of the Stars and Stripes is created following the admission of the 25th state, Arkansas, into the Union.
July 4, 1837	The eighth official design of the Stars and Stripes is created when the 26th star is added to designate the admittance of Michigan into the Union.
1841	The U.S. Army authorizes the use of the Stars and Stripes by the infantry.
July 4, 1845	The ninth official design of the Stars and Stripes (27 stars) is created following the admission of Florida to the Union.
July 4, 1846	The 10th official design of the Stars and Stripes is created by the addition of the 28th star, to signify the admittance of Texas into the Union.
July 4, 1847	Iowa's star brings the total to 29, creating the 11th official design of the national flag.
July 4, 1848	The 12th official design of the Stars and Stripes is created with the admission of Wisconsin into the Union. The flag consists of 30 stars.
July 4, 1851	The 13th official design of the American flag is created with the admission of California into the Union. The new flag includes 31 stars.
1853	The Stars and Stripes is displayed in Japan for the first time, taken there by the U.S. Navy.
July 4, 1858	The 14th official design of the American flag is created by adding the 32nd star to mark the admittance of Minnesota into the Union.
July 4, 1859	The addition of the 33rd star, recognizing the admittance of Oregon into the Union, creates the 15th official design of the Stars and Stripes.
June 14, 1861	The first recorded local observance of Flag Day, the anniversary of the First Flag Law, takes place at Hartford, Connecticut.

April 12, 1861	The Civil War begins with Confederate fire on Fort Sumter, South Carolina. The fort surrenders the next day, striking the Stars and Stripes.
July 4, 1861	The 34th star is added to the flag for the admittance of Kansas into the Union, creating the 16th official design.
July 4, 1863	The 17th official design of the Stars and Stripes comes into being with the addition of the 35th star, recognizing the admittance of West Virginia into the Union.
July 4, 1865	Nevada's star is added to the Stars and Stripes, creating a 36-star flag and the 18th official design.
November 1871	The Stars and Stripes is carried into the interior of Africa for the first time when newspaperman Henry Stanley goes in search of Dr. David Livingstone.
July 4, 1877	The centennial of the First Flag Act sees the 38th star added for the admission of Colorado into the Union, creating the 20th official design of the Stars and Stripes.
June 14, 1885	Bernard Cigrand, a Wisconsin school teacher, arranges for his students to celebrate the day as the flag's birthday. He is later given credit for helping to promote Flag Day.
July 4, 1890	The 21st official design of the Stars and Stripes is created with the addition of five stars: for North Dakota, South Dakota, Washington, Idaho and Montana. The union of the new American flag now consists of 43 stars.
July 4, 1891	A 44th star is added to the flag for the admission of Wyoming into the Union, creating the 22nd official design of the Stars and Stripes.
September 8, 1892	The first version of the "Pledge of Allegiance" is published in a children's magazine, the *Youth's Companion*.
July 4, 1896	The 23rd official design of the Stars and stripes is created by the addition of the 45th star, which represents the admittance of Utah into the Union.
February 15, 1898	The battleship *Maine* is sunk in the harbor at Havana, Cuba. Her flag is later recovered.
February 20, 1905	Congress passes the first federal law on flag protocol, prohibiting the use of the Stars and Stripes in trademarks.
July 4, 1908	The 46th star is added to the flag in recognition of Oklahoma's admission to the Union, creating the 24th official design of the Stars and Stripes.
April 6, 1909	Admiral Robert E. Peary places the Stars and Stripes at the North Pole.
September 7, 1911	The Stars and Stripes leaves New York City on its first transcontinental airplane flight. It arrives in Pasadena, California, on November 5, 1911, after 82 hours and 4 minutes of actual flight time.

June 24, 1912	The first official specifications of design and dimensions for the U.S. flag are issued by President Howard Taft.
July 4, 1912	The 25th official design of the Stars and Stripes is created with the addition of the 47th and 48th stars for the admission of New Mexico and Arizona into the Union. This flag is used for 47 years, the longest period of time for the Stars and Stripes to remain unchanged in design.
June 14, 1916	The first Flag Day is observed by presidential proclamation.
November 11, 1923	The world's largest flag is displayed in Detroit, Michigan, by the J.L. Hudson Company. It is 236 feet long and 104 feet wide. Each star is six feet tall, and each stripe is eight feet wide. A new 50-star flag of the same dimensions is displayed by the same company on March 2, 1960.
September 28, 1924	The Stars and Stripes completes its first trip around the world by air. The trip began on April 6.
June 13, 1927	The flag is displayed from the right hand of the Statue of Liberty in honor of U.S. aviator Charles Lindbergh.
November 29, 1929	Admiral Richard Byrd carries the Stars and Stripes to Little America in Antarctica, the southernmost point on Earth.
March 3, 1931	President Herbert Hoover signs into law a bill making the "Star-Spangled Banner" the national anthem of the United States.
November 20, 1933	The Stars and Stripes travels in a Navy balloon to a record altitude of 61,237 feet.
August 11, 1934	The flag descends 2,510 feet under the surface of the ocean and returns with Dr. William Beebe and Otis Barton, establishing a world diving record.
May 7, 1937	Pennsylvania becomes the first state to recognize Flag Day as a legal day of observance.
1942	Congress adopts the "Pledge of Allegiance" and the Flag Code, as recommended by the Flag Conference in 1923 and 1924, as federal law.
August 3, 1949	President Harry Truman designates June 14 as Flag Day, formally approving a national day of observance that has been honored to some extent since the Civil War.
July 4, 1959	The 26th official design of the Stars and Stripes is created with the addition of the 49th star, recognizing the admittance of Alaska into the Union.
July 4, 1960	The 50th star is added to the American flag in recognition of Hawaii being admitted into the Union, creating the 27th official design of the national flag. A 50-star flag is hoisted at 12:01 A.M. over Fort McHenry near Baltimore by presidential order to honor the victory described in the "Star-Spangled Banner."

May 6, 1961	The Stars and Stripes reaches outer space with astronaut Alan Shepard, the first American in space.
July 10, 1962	The American Telstar satellite broadcasts its first picture from outer space, the Stars and Stripes. It is televised around the world while the American national anthem is played.
May 1, 1963	The Stars and Stripes reaches the highest point on Earth when American James Whittaker imbeds a pole atop Mount Everest in Nepal and attaches the American flag.
January 9-17, 1964	The flying of the Stars and Stripes over a high school for American dependents in the Panama Canal Zone brings about rioting between Panamanians and Americans, resulting in the loss of 25 lives.
July 1968	Congress passes the first federal law providing punishment for the desecration of the national flag.
July 21, 1969	Astronauts Neil Armstrong and Edwin Aldrin plant the Stars and Stripes on the moon. The occasion marks the longest distance from home that the American flag has been displayed. Attached to an embedded flagpole, the flag has a wire run through its top to make the fabric stand out in the lack of atmosphere. Unless repositioned or removed by other visitors to the moon, the Stars and Stripes will remain as positioned by the astronauts indefinitely.
June 14, 1983	The world's largest flag — 411 by 210 feet and named the "Great American Flag" — is unfurled in Washington, D.C., in honor of Flag Day. The flag is made of nylon strapped together with seat-belt fabric. It weighs seven tons.

Admittance of States into the Union by Date and Flag Design

State	Date Admitted	Official Design Number
Delaware	*December 7, 1787	1st Design/13 Stars
Pennsylvania	*December 12, 1787	1st Design/13 Stars
New Jersey	*December 18, 1787	1st Design/13 Stars
Georgia	*January 2, 1788	1st Design/13 Stars
Connecticut	*January 9, 1788	1st Design/13 Stars
Massachusetts	*February 6, 1788	1st Design/13 Stars
Maryland	*April 28, 1788	1st Design/13 Stars
South Carolina	*May 23, 1788	1st Design/13 Stars
New Hampshire	*June 21, 1788	1st Design/13 Stars
Virginia	*June 25, 1788	1st Design/13 Stars
New York	*July 25, 1788	1st Design/13 Stars
North Carolina	*November 21, 1789	1st Design/13 Stars
Rhode Island	May 29, 1790	1st Design/13 Stars
Vermont	March 4, 1791	**2nd Design/15 Stars
Kentucky	June 1, 1792	**2nd Design/15 Stars
Tennessee	June 1, 1796	**2nd Design/15 Stars
Ohio	March 1, 1803	**2nd Design/15 Stars
Louisiana	April 30, 1812	**2nd Design/15 Stars
Indiana	December 11, 1816	**2nd Design/15 Stars
Mississippi	December 10, 1817	3rd Design/20 Stars

Illinois	December 3, 1818	4th Design/21 Stars
Alabama	December 14, 1819	5th Design/22 Stars
Maine	March 15, 1820	5th Design/23 Stars
Missouri	August 10, 1821	6th Design/24 Stars
Arkansas	June 15, 1836	7th Design/25 Stars
Michigan	January 26, 1837	8th Design/26 Stars
Florida	March 3, 1845	9th Design/27 Stars
Texas	December 29, 1845	10th Design/28 Stars
Iowa	December 26, 1846	11th Design/29 Stars
Wisconsin	May 29, 1848	12th Design/30 Stars
California	September 9, 1850	13th Design/31 Stars
Minnesota	May 11, 1858	14th Design/32 Stars
Oregon	February 14, 1859	15th Design/33 Stars
Kansas	January 23, 1861	16th Design/34 Stars
West Virginia	June 20, 1863	17th Design/35 Stars
Nevada	October 31, 1864	18th Design/36 Stars
Nebraska	March 1, 1867	19th Design/37 Stars
Colorado	August 1, 1876	20th Design/38 Stars
North Dakota	November 2, 1889	21st Design/43 Stars
South Dakota	November 2, 1889	21st Design/43 Stars
Montana	November 3, 1889	21st Design/43 Stars
Washington	November 11, 1889	21st Design/43 Stars
Idaho	July 3, 1890	21st Design/43 Stars
Wyoming	July 10, 1890	22nd Design/44 Stars
Utah	January 4, 1896	23rd Design/45 Stars
Oklahoma	November 16, 1907	24th Design/46 Stars
New Mexico	January 6, 1912	25th Design/48 Stars
Arizona	February 14, 1912	25th Design/48 Stars
Alaska	January 3, 1959	26th Design/49 Stars
Hawaii	August 21, 1959	27th Design/50 Stars

*Denotes the days the first 13 colonies ratified the Constitution of the United States.
**Denotes the only official flag of the United States containing 15 stripes.

Flag Codes and Rules

★

THE U.S. ARMED SERVICES were the first to issue specific regulations to ensure that proper respect would be shown to the national flag. Civilians had no formal rules to follow and relied upon their common sense, tradition or accepted local customs. It was not until 146 years from the time of the First Flag Resolution that a consolidated effort was undertaken to provide a set of rules concerning the American flag.

On June 14, 1923, representatives of more than 60 civic and patriotic groups met in Washington, D.C., to draft a uniform code of flag etiquette. They agreed to adopt almost entirely a War Department circular issued four months earlier on February 15 as a civilian code for the use and care of the national flag.

Nineteen years later, Congress adopted the code, as it had been set forth by the representatives, as federal law. It was approved by President Franklin D. Roosevelt on December 22, 1942.

As with any resolution or bill passed by Congress and accepted by the President, the Flag Code is subject to change through normal judicial channels. However, the commander in chief of the armed forces of the United States, the president, has the power to alter, repeal, modify or add rules to the Flag Code "whenever he deems it to be appropriate or desirable; and any such alteration or additional rule shall be set forth in a proclamation." This power has yet to be used.

The Flag Code adopted in 1942 by the federal government is still in use with only a few minor changes. There are no federal penalties for violations of the code, even though it is federal law. Any or all penalties for violations of the Flag Code by citizens other than military personnel are imposed by individual states.

The following are simplified and abbreviated excerpts of the Flag Code.

Display of the flag

It is customary to display the flag either from buildings or flagstaffs in the open from sunrise to sunset only. When a patriotic effect is desired, the flag may be displayed 24 hours a day if properly illuminated during darkness.

The flag should be hoisted briskly and lowered ceremoniously. The flag should not be displayed in bad weather unless an all-weather flag is used.

The flag should be displayed on all days, but particularly on:

New Year's Day	January 1
Inauguration Day	January 20
Lincoln's Birthday	February 12
Washington's Birthday	Third Monday in February
Easter Sunday	Variable
Mother's Day	Second Sunday in May
Armed Forces Day	Third Saturday in May
Memorial Day *(half-staff until noon)*	Last Monday in May
Flag Day	June 14
Independence Day	July 4
Labor Day	First Monday in September
Constitution Day	September 17
Columbus Day	Second Monday in October
Navy Day	October 27
Veteran's Day	November 11
Thanksgiving Day	Fourth Thursday in November
Christmas Day	December 25

The flag should also be displayed on state holidays of the state in which you reside (including the date of its admission to the Union) and other days proclaimed by the president of the United States.

The flag should be displayed on or near the main administration building of every public institution.

The flag should be displayed in or near every polling place on election days.

The flag should be displayed during school days in or near every schoolhouse.

The flag, when carried in a procession with another flag or flags, should be displayed either on the marching right (the flag's own right) or, in a line of flags, in front of the center of that line.

The flag should not be displayed on a float in a parade except from a staff.

The flag should not be draped over the hood, top, sides or back of a vehicle, railroad train or boat. When displayed on a car, the flag should be fixed to a staff firmly attached to the chassis or clamped to the right fender.

No other flag or pennant should be placed above the U.S. flag except during church services conducted by naval chaplains at sea for Navy personnel, when the church pennant may be flown above the American flag. When placed on the same level with other flags or pennants, the American flag should be to the right. No other flag should be given a position of superior prominence or honor to the U.S. flag at any place within the United States, its territories and/or possessions.

When displayed against a wall from crossed staffs with another flag, the American flag should be to its right with its staff in front of the other flag's staff.

When displayed with state flags or pennants of societies on staffs, the U.S. flag should be at the center and at the highest point of the group.

The U.S. flag should always be at the top of a halyard when flown with flags of states, cities or localities or with pennants of societies. If flown from adjacent staffs, the U.S. flag should be hoisted first and lowered last. No flag or pennant may be placed higher or to the right of the U.S. flag.

Flags of two or more nations are to be flown from separate staffs of equal heights, with each flag being about equal in size in time of peace.

When displayed from a staff projecting horizontally, the union of the flag should be placed at the peak of the staff unless the flag is at half-staff. If suspended over a sidewalk from a rope extending from a house to a pole at the edge of the sidewalk, the flag should be hoisted out union-first from the building.

When displayed either horizontally or vertically against a wall, the union should be uppermost and to the flag's own right. The flag should be displayed in the same fashion in a window.

The flag should be displayed over the middle of a street by suspending it vertically with the union to the north in an east-west street or to the east in a north-south street.

When displayed flat on a speaker platform, the flag should be above and behind the speaker. When displayed from a staff in a church or public auditorium, the flag should be in advance of the audience and to the speaker's right as he faces the audience. Any other flags present should be placed to the left of the speaker.

When suspended across a corridor or lobby in a building with one main entrance, the flag should be vertical with the union facing the observer's left upon entering. If the building has more than one main entrance, the flag should be suspended vertically near the center of the corridor or lobby. The union should face north when the main entrances face east and west, and east when the main entrances face north and south. If the main entrances encompass more than two directions, the flag's union should always face east.

When the flag is used to cover a casket, it should be draped with the union at the head and over the left shoulder. The flag should not be lowered into the grave. The flag should not be allowed to touch the ground.

At the unveiling ceremony of a statue or monument, the flag should be a distinctive feature, but never a cover.

It is not improper to display outdated flags.

Displaying the flag at half-staff

When flown at half-staff, the flag first should be hoisted to the peak for an instant before lowering to the half-staff position. The flag should be raised to the peak again before lowering.

The flag should be displayed at half-staff only until noon on Memorial Day.

The flag should be displayed at half-staff for a 30-day period after the death of a president or former president.

The flag should be displayed at half-staff for a 10-day period after the death of a vice president, chief justice of the United States, or speaker of the House of Representatives.

The flag should be displayed at half-staff from the day of death until interment for an associate justice of the Supreme Court, a secretary of an executive department, secretary of a military department, former vice president, governor of a state, governor of a territory, or governor of a U.S. possession.

The flag should be displayed at half-staff on the day of death and the following day for a member of Congress.

The flag should be displayed at half-staff upon the death of any other officials or foreign dignitaries, according to presidential instructions or in accordance with recognized customs and practices not inconsistent with the law.

The governor of a state, territory or possession may proclaim that the flag shall be flown at half-staff at the death of a present or former official of his state, territory or possession.

Respect for the flag

No disrespect should be shown to the flag of the United States. The flag should not be dipped to any person or thing. Regimental colors, state flags and organizational or institutional flags are to be dipped as a mark of honor.

The flag should never be displayed with the union down, except as a signal of distress in instances of extreme danger to life or property.

The flag should never touch anything beneath it, such as the ground, floor, water or merchandise.

The flag should never be carried flat or horizontally, but always aloft and free.

The flag should never be used as wearing apparel, bedding or drapery. It should never be festooned, drawn back or up, but always allowed to fall free. Bunting of blue, white and red — always arranged with the blue above the white in the middle and the red below — should be used for covering a speaker's desk, draping the front of the platform, and for decoration in general. The flag should never be fastened, displayed, used or stored in such a manner as to permit it to be easily torn, soiled or damaged.

The flag should never be used as a covering for a ceiling.

The flag should never be placed upon any part of, nor attached to, any mark, insignia, letter, word, figure, design, picture or drawing of any nation.

The flag should never be used as a receptacle for receiving, holding, carrying or delivering anything.

The flag should never be used for advertising purposes in any manner whatsoever. It should not be embroidered on such articles as cushions or handkerchiefs and the like, printed or otherwise impressed on paper napkins or boxes, or anything that is designed for temporary use and disposal. Advertising signs should not be fastened to a staff or halyard from which the flag is flown.

No part of the flag should ever be used as a costume or athletic uniform. However, a flag patch may be affixed to the uniform of military personnel, firemen, policemen and members of patriotic organizations. The flag represents a living country and is itself considered a living thing. Therefore, the lapel flag pin, being a replica, should be worn on the left lapel near the heart.

Soiled flags may be renovated by either washing or dry cleaning. Worn-out flags should be destroyed in a dignified manner, preferably by burning.

Conduct during hoisting, lowering or passing of the flag

During the ceremony of hoisting or lowering the flag, or when the flag is passing in a parade or in review, all persons present except those in uniform should face the flag and stand at attention with the right hand over the heart. Those present in uniform should stand and render the military salute. When not in uniform, men should remove their headdress with the right hand and hold it at the left shoulder, the hand being over the heart. Aliens should stand at attention. The salute to the flag in a moving column should be rendered at the moment the flag passes.

Prohibition on trademarks

The first federal law prohibiting the use of the American flag in a registered trademark was passed in 1905. In 1946, the law was amended to read that a trademark could not be registered if it "consists of or compromises the flag or coat of arms or other insignia of the United States or of any State or municipality, or of any foreign nation, or any simulation thereof."

Changes of design in the flag

The design of the U.S. flag can be altered only by an act of Congress or presidential order. When Alaska's statehood was assured in 1958, President Eisenhower appointed a flag committee of five members to arrange the 49 stars in the canton. A similar procedure was followed in designing the 50-star flag with the admission of Hawaii to the Union.

Glossary

Banner	Originally a large, rectangular medieval flag, usually carried into battle. In modern times, it refers to any rectangular piece of fabric used as a symbol; i.e., a flag or standard.
Canton	Originally a word describing the four quarters of a shield and always less than one-quarter of the total surface of a flag. In modern times, as used on flags, it is the area in the top corner next to the pole or staff. In the national flag representing the United States, it refers to the union.
Colors	Originally the colors used in national flags, badges, etc. In modern times, it is often used to mean the actual flag.
Dip	To lower a flag slightly and immediately raise it again as a form of salute. NOTE: The Stars and Stripes should never be dipped to any person or flag.
Ensign	Originally a standard, badge, emblem, symbol or sign. In modern America, it is a flag at sea. It may also be a military or naval flag or banner.
Field	The flag surface that functions as a background. The Stars and Stripes has a blue field in the canton, with the balance of the field comprised of horizontal red and white stripes.
Flagpole	A permanent pole for flying the flag.
Flagstaff	A movable pole that can be carried and is used for displaying a flag.
Fly	The length of the flag from left to right. Also, the area of the flag farthest from the staff or pole.
Ground	The background color of a flag or any of its parts. Also known as the field.
Half-mast	The display of a flag at a point some distance, but not necessarily halfway down, a flagpole or flagstaff. It is a display of mourning.

Half-staff	A term interchangeable with "half-mast."
Halyard	Ropes or lines used to raise and lower a flag.
Hoist	The height of the flag from the top to the bottom. Also, the area of the flag closest to the pole or staff.
Hoist the colors/flag	The act of raising a flag.
Jack	A naval flag smaller than an ensign and flown at a ship's bow as a mark of distinction or to show nationality. The American Jack is the canton of the Stars and Stripes, a blue field containing 50 five-pointed stars.
National flag	The official flag of a country or nation. The national flag of the United States is often referred to as the American flag or the Stars and Stripes.
Peak	The highest point a flag can reach on a pole or staff.
Pennant	A narrow, tapering flag originally used as an emblem or symbol. In the United States, it is more commonly used as a military flag.
Standard	A term interchangeable with "pennant."
Strike the colors	The act of lowering a flag in surrender or defeat.
Union	The combining of two or more nations or flags into one flag. In the flag of Great Britain, the union is a combination of the St. George Cross, the St. Andrew Cross and the St. Patrick Cross. In the American flag, the union refers to the canton, or the union of the states represented by the stars.

Suggested Reading

Carmichael, John H. *Stars and Stripes: The Complete Story of Our Flag*. New York: Gladstone Press, 1971.

Crampton, William G. *Flags of the United States*. New York: W. H. Smith, 1989.

Eggenberger, David. *Flags of the United States of America*. New York: Thomas Y. Crowell Co., 1959.

Flagg, Robert. *Our 83 Flags*. Houston: Southwest Savings Association, 1963.

Furlong, William Rea. *So Proudly We Hail: The History of the United States Flag*. Washington, D.C.: Smithsonian Institution Press, 1981.

Grove, Maria Louise. *The Evolution of the Flag*. Austin: University of Texas Press, 1973.

Linton, Calvin D., ed. *The Bicentennial Almanac*. Nashville: Thomas Nelson, Inc., 1975.

Manwaring, David R. *Render Unto Caesar*. Chicago: University of Chicago Press, 1962.

Mastai, Boleslow, and Marie-Louise D. Mastai. *The Stars and Stripes*. New York: Alfred A. Knopf, 1973.

Parrish, Thomas D. *The American Flag*. New York: Simon & Schuster, 1973.

Quaife, Milo Milton. *The History of the United States Flag, From the Revolution to the Present, Including a Guide to Its Use and Display*. New York: Harper & Brothers, 1961.

Werstein, Irving. *The Stars and Stripes: The Story of Our Flag*. New York: Golden Press, 1969.